Active Experiences for Active Children

SOCIAL STUDIES

SECOND EDITION

Carol Seefeldt

Alice Galper

PEARSON

Merrill
Prentice Hall

Upper Saddle River, New Jersey
Columbus, Ohio

Library of Congress Cataloging-in-Publication Data

Seefeldt, Carol.
   Active experiences for active children: social studies/Carol Seefeldt, Alice Galper.--2nd ed.
      p. cm.
   Includes bibliographical references and index.
   ISBN 0-13-170748-5
   1. Social sciences--study and teaching (Early childhood)--United States. 2. Early childhood education--Activity programs--United
States. 3. Active learning--United States. I. Title: Social studies. II. Galper, Alice. III. Title.
   LB1139.5.S64S44 2006
   372.83--dc22

Vice President and Executive Publisher: Jeffery W. Johnston
Publisher: Kevin M. Davis
Editor: Julie Peters
Editorial Assistant: Michelle Girgis
Production Editor: Sheryl Glicker Langner
Production Coordination: Lea Baranowski, Carlisle Publishers Services
Design Coordinator: Diane C. Lorenzo
Photo Coordinator: Monica Merkel
Cover Design: Ali Mohrman
Production Manager: Laura Messerly
Director of Marketing: Ann Castel Davis
Marketing Manager: Amy Judd
Marketing Coordinator: Brian Mounts

This book was set in Times by Carlisle Communications, Ltd. It was printed and bound by Edwards Brothers Malloy

Photo Credits: David Mager/Pearson Learning Photo Studio, pp. 3, 15, 21, 41, 107; Pearson Learning Photo Studio, pp. 6, 17, 165,
172; Richard Farcus, pp. 11, 73; Todd Yarrington/Merrill, p. 29; Silver Burdett Ginn, p. 32; Timothy P. Dingman/PH College, p. 35;
Scott Cunningham/Merrill, p. 45; Anthony Magnacca/Merrill, pp. 48, 67, 76, 140, 159; Laima Druskis/PH College, pp. 51, 87;
Ken Karp/PH College, p. 54; © Pearson Scott Foresman, p. 58; Kenneth P. Davis/PH College, p. 85; EMG Education Management
Group, p. 97; Anne Vega/Merrill, pp. 108, 112, 142, 151; Barbara Schwartz/Merrill, pp. 121, 124; Shirley Zeiberg/PH College,
pp. 126, 135; Teri Stratford/PH College, p. 152; Mike Peters/Silver Burdett Ginn, p. 170.

Pearson Education Ltd.
Pearson Education Singapore Pte. Ltd.
Pearson Education Canada, Ltd.
Pearson Education—Japan

Pearson Education Australia Pty. Limited
Pearson Education North Asia Ltd.
Pearson Educación de Mexico, S.A. de C.V.
Pearson Education Malaysia Pte. Ltd.

20 19 18 17 16 15 14 13
ISBN: 0-13-170748-5

Dedication

◆   *Active Experiences for Active Children: Social Studies,* Second Edition, is dedicated to Carol Seefeldt, who died on January 5, 2005, during the revision of the book. Carol was a brilliant scholar, a great writer, and a wonderful colleague and friend. The social studies were her favorite topics because she believed so strongly in democracy and working with children to be active participants in a democratic society.

Alice Galper

Educator Learning Center: An Invaluable Online Resource

Merrill Education and the Association for Supervision and Curriculum Development (ASCD) invite you to take advantage of a new online resource, one that provides access to the top research and proven strategies associated with ASCD and Merrill—the Educator Learning Center. At **www.educatorlearningcenter.com**, you will find resources that will enhance your students' understanding of course topics and of current educational issues, in addition to being invaluable for further research.

HOW THE EDUCATOR LEARNING CENTER WILL HELP YOUR STUDENTS BECOME BETTER TEACHERS

With the combined resources of Merrill Education and ASCD, you and your students will find a wealth of tools and materials to better prepare them for the classroom.

Research

- More than 600 articles from the ASCD journal *Educational Leadership* discuss everyday issues faced by practicing teachers.
- A direct link on the site to Research Navigator™ gives students access to many of the leading education journals, as well as extensive content detailing the research process.
- Excerpts from Merrill Education texts give your students insights on important topics of instructional methods, diverse populations, assessment, classroom management, technology, and refining classroom practice.

Classroom Practice

- Hundreds of lesson plans and teaching strategies are categorized by content area and age range.
- Case studies and classroom video footage provide virtual field experience for student reflection.
- Computer simulations and other electronic tools keep your students abreast of today's classrooms and current technologies.

LOOK INTO THE VALUE OF EDUCATOR LEARNING CENTER YOURSELF

A four-month subscription to Educator Learning Center is $25 but is **FREE** when packaged with any Merrill Education text. In order for your students to have access to this site, you must use this special value-pack ISBN number **WHEN** placing your textbook order with the bookstore: 0-13-154960-X. Your students will then receive a copy of the text packaged with a free ASCD pincode. To preview the value of this website to you and your students, please go to **www.educatorlearningcenter.com** and click on "Demo."

Preface

"What can I do tomorrow?" teachers ask. "And I don't mean just another meaningless activity. I need something that will keep children involved and lead to successful learning." Grounded in John Dewey's philosophy that all genuine education comes through experience but that not all experiences are equally educative, *Active Experiences for Active Children: Social Studies* answers teachers' questions about what to do tomorrow.

In this book, teachers will learn how to plan and implement meaningful thematic experiences that truly educate young children, not just keep them busy. Teachers are given guides to planning and implementing a curriculum that will lead to a high level of involvement on the part of children and to children's academic success.

NEW FEATURES IN THIS EDITION

This revised edition has several new additions. Chapter 5, "Different Kinds of Families," has been added to Part Two. Each of the Experiences chapters has been carefully organized around the integrated standards enunciated by the National Council for the Social Studies, which are clearly spelled out in Part One. This allows teachers to know which standards they are meeting with a particular objective or activity. In addition, Goals and Objectives for children at the beginning of the Experiences chapters are based on key concepts from the various disciplines that make up the social studies. The book has been substantially expanded with updated and additional resources and activities.

MEANINGFUL EXPERIENCES

Active Experiences for Active Children: Social Studies consists of clear, concise, usable guides for planning meaningful learning experiences in the social studies for children in childcare settings, preschool programs, Head Start, and kindergarten. Primary-grade children can engage in active experiential learning as well, and each experience is extended to the early primary grades (grades 1–3).

The experiences in this book are meaningful because they

- are grounded in children's interests and needs and in their here-and-now world

- have integrity in terms of content key to the subjects that make up the social studies

- involve children in group work or projects

- have continuity: One experience builds on another, forming a complete, coherent, integrated learning curriculum for young children as well as connecting the early childhood setting to children's homes and communities

- promote the skills and attitudes children will need not only to participate in our democratic society, but to continually improve that society

- provide time and opportunity for children to think and reflect on their experiences
- are based on the key concepts and themes identified by experts in the social studies

AUDIENCE

This book is designed for pre- and in-service teachers of young children. It is suitable as a core or supplemental text in community college and four-year college or university early childhood courses. Although heavily based in theory, its practicality will also be ideal for teachers who desire the best for young children but have limited training or formal preparation. Professionals working in childcare, Head Start, or other early childhood settings will find that *Active Experiences for Active Children: Social Studies* supports their growth and understanding of how to put theory into practice. When used in conjunction with the other three *Active Experiences* books (Science, Math, and Literacy), it provides a complete curriculum for the early childhood classroom.

ORGANIZATION

Part One, which includes the first four chapters, describes how to plan and implement experiential learning. Chapter 1 discusses the standards that give direction and guidance to planning curriculum for young children. Part Two includes the eight Experiences chapters, each of which contains a "For the Teacher" section. These sections include tear-out sheets for parents, planning, and evaluation, as well as resources and other information teachers need to implement the suggested activities. Each Experiences chapter also includes a "For the Child" section. In these sections continuous learning experiences, activities, and ideas for teaching are illustrated. This edition contains extensive references to children's books, Web resources, and books for teachers.

There are numerous activity books on the market. Many, however, present isolated activities that are often meaningless to children and void of any real content or learning potential. *Active Experiences for Active Children: Social Studies* offers teachers an integrated approach to planning curriculum for young children. Because it is based on key concepts from discipline areas of the social studies, reflecting current research and theories, the book not only has intellectual integrity but uniqueness as well. Then, too, no activity books on the market deal with preparing children to be full participants in a democratic society as is done here.

The expertise and background of the authors is another important feature of this text. Together the authors bring a unique perspective to the book. Both experienced Deweyan education. Both worked in Head Start, childcare, and other early childhood settings and thus bring an intimate knowledge of practice to the text. Because both were researchers, the latest in theory and research in the field of early childhood education is represented in the text.

ACKNOWLEDGMENTS

Carol Seefeldt died in January 2005, but she would join me in thanking Julie Peters, who was patient and understanding during the revision of this book and was responsible for suggesting many of the updates that contribute to making the revised edition a better book for teachers and children. Ann Davis, our original editor, contributed her extensive knowledge of early childhood education in the development of the first edition. We appreciate the expertise and careful attention of Lea Baranowski, Michelle Girgis, Sheryl Langner, and Monica Merkel.

We would like to thank the following reviewers for their valuable suggestions and comments: Susan Matoba Adler, University of Illinois at Urbana-Champaign; JoAnne Buggey, University of Minnesota; Marjorie Krebs, Bowling Green State University; Mary Larue, J. Sargeant Reynolds Community College; and Rahima Wade, University of Iowa.

I know Carol would have insisted on acknowledging her late husband, Gene Seefeldt, for believing that women can accomplish great things. Thanks to Harvey Galper, whose economic expertise was valuable in the shaping of economic experiences for children. I am further grateful to my many colleagues who helped to fill the gap left by Carol's death.

Alice Galper

Discover the Companion Website Accompanying This Book

THE PRENTICE HALL COMPANION WEBSITE: A VIRTUAL LEARNING ENVIRONMENT

Technology is a constantly growing and changing aspect of our field that is creating a need for content and resources. To address this emerging need, Prentice Hall has developed an online learning environment for students and professors alike—Companion Websites—to support our textbooks.

In creating a Companion Website, our goal is to build on and enhance what the textbook already offers. For this reason, the content for each user-friendly website is organized by topic and provides the professor and student with a variety of meaningful resources. Common features of a Companion Website include:

For the Professor—

Every Companion Website integrates **Syllabus Manager**™, an online syllabus creation and management utility.

- **Syllabus Manager**™ provides you, the instructor, with an easy, step-by-step process to create and revise syllabi, with direct links into the Companion Website and other online content without having to learn HTML.

- Students may log on to your syllabus during any study session. All they need to know is the web address for the Companion Website and the password you've assigned to your syllabus.

- After you have created a syllabus using **Syllabus Manager**™, students may enter the syllabus for their course section from any point in the Companion Website.

- Clicking on a date, the student is shown the list of activities for the assignment. The activities for each assignment are linked directly to actual content, saving time for students.

- Adding assignments consists of clicking on the desired due date, then filling in the details of the assignment—name of the assignment, instructions, and whether it is a one-time or repeating assignment.

- In addition, links to other activities can be created easily. If the activity is online, a URL can be entered in the space provided, and it will be linked automatically in the final syllabus.

- Your completed syllabus is hosted on our servers, allowing convenient updates from any computer on the Internet. Changes you make to your syllabus are immediately available to your students at their next logon.

For the Student—

- **Introduction**—General information about the topic and how it will be covered in the website.

- **Web Links**—A variety of websites related to topic areas.

- **Timely Articles**—Links to online articles that enable you to become more aware of important issues in early childhood.

- **Learn by Doing**—Put concepts into action, participate in activities, examine strategies, and more.

- **Visit a School**—Visit a school's website to see concepts, theories, and strategies in action.

- **For Teachers/Practitioners**—Access information you will need to know as an educator, including information on materials, activities, and lessons.

- **Observation Tools**—A collection of checklists and forms to print and use when observing and assessing children's development.

- **Current Policies and Standards**—Find out the latest early childhood policies from the government and various organizations, and view state, federal, and curriculum standards.

- **Resources and Organizations**—Discover tools to help you plan your classroom or center and organizations to provide current information and standards for each topic.

- **Electronic Bluebook**—Paperless method of completing homework or essays assigned by a professor. Finished work can be sent to the professor via e-mail.

- **Message Board**—Virtual bulletin board to post and respond to questions and comments from a national audience.

To take advantage of these resources, please visit Merrill Education's *Early Childhood Education Resources* website. Go to **www.prenhall.com/seefeldt**, click on the book cover, and then click on "Enter" at the bottom of the next screen.

Contents

PART ONE
Theory of Active Experiences 1

1 Experiences and Education: Putting Dewey's Theory Into Practice 3

Deep Personal Meaning 4
  Firsthand Experience 4
  Initiative, Choices, and Decision Making 5
  Age Appropriateness 6
Content with Integrity and Meaning 7
Involving Others 9
  Play 9
  Group Work and Projects 9
  Interactions with Teachers and Other Adults 10
Covered with Language 10
Continuity of Learning 11
Time to Reflect 12
  Organizing 12
  Evaluating 13
Summary 13

2 Active Children—Active Environments 15

The Essentials: Health, Safety, Inclusion, and Beauty 16
  Health and Safety 16
  Planning for Inclusion 17
  Beauty 18
Indoor Spaces 18
  Art Centers 18
  Book and Library Centers 19
  Sociodramatic Play Areas 20
  Areas for Manipulatives 21

Science Areas 21
Block Areas 22
Water and Sand Areas 22
Music/Movement Areas 22
Computer Stations 23
Quiet Spaces 23
Cooking Spaces 23

Outdoor Spaces 23

Physical Activity 24

Other Outdoor Activity 25

Sociodramatic Play 25
Art 25
Science 25
Music 26
Math 26
Organized Games 26

The Teacher's Role 26

Summary 27

3 Building Connections to Home and Community Through Active Experiences 29

Out Into the School 31

Persons in the Immediate Environment 31
Inside the School Building 32
Outside in the Natural Environment 32

Out Into the Neighborhood and Community 33

Basic Guidelines for Meaningful Field Experiences 33

Safety Tips for Field Experiences 34

Building Connections with the Neighborhood and Community 35

For Democracy 35
For Diversity 36

The Home-School Connection 39

Summary 40

4 Experiences and Social Studies Content 41

Knowledge of Children 42

Three-Year-Olds 42
Four-Year-Olds 43
Five-Year-Olds 43

Knowledge of the Subject Matter—The Social Studies 43

Bringing Knowledge of Children and Content Together 45

Expanding and Extending Firsthand Experiences 46

Summary 48

PART TWO
Guides to Active Experiences   49

5   Different Kinds of Families   51

For the Teacher   52

What You'll Need to Know   52
Key Concepts, Goals, and Objectives Based on CTB and
  Curriculum Standards for the Social Studies   53
What You'll Need   53
The Home-School Connection   55
Evaluating and Assessing Children's Learning   56

For the Children   56

Standard 1. Understanding What Families Do   56
Standard 2. Learning and Describing the Unique Features
  of Different Families   57
Standard 3. Children Will Form Positive Relationships with Children
  from Different Kinds of Families   59
Reflecting   61
Extending and Expanding to the Primary Grades   62
Documenting Children's Learning   63

6   The Past Is Present: History for Young Children   67

For the Teacher   68

What You'll Need to Know   68
History Standards: Key Concepts   68
Goals and Objectives   68
What You'll Need   69
The Home-School Connection   70
Evaluating and Assessing Children's Learning   70

For the Children   71

Standard 1. Measuring the Passage of Time   71
Standard 2. Learning About Past, Present, and Future Time   72
Standard 3. Learning to Record the Changes That Occur
  with the Passage of Time   74
Standard 4. Using the Methods of the Historian: Observing, Collecting Data,
  Reflecting, and Reaching Conclusions   76
Reflecting and Reaching Conclusions   77
Extending and Expanding to the Early Primary Grades   78
Documenting Children's Learning   79

7   Earth: The Place We Live   85

For the Teacher   86

What You'll Need to Know   86
Geography Standards: Key Concepts   86

Goals and Objectives   86
What You'll Need   87

Sand and Water for Children with Special Needs   88

The Home-School Connection   89
Evaluating and Assessing Children's Learning   89

For the Children   90

Standard 1. The Earth Is a Part of the Solar System   90
Standard 2. The Earth Is Covered with Different Surfaces   91
Standard 3. Each Place Has Unique Characteristics   94
Standard 4. A Wide Variety of Plants and Animals Live on the Earth   95
Reflecting   96
Extending and Expanding to the Early Primary Grades   96

Time to Pretend   96

Documenting Children's Learning   97

8 Mapping for Young Children   107

For the Teacher   108

What You'll Need to Know   108
Mapping Standards   108
Goals and Objectives   109
What You'll Need   109
The Home-School Connection   110
Evaluating and Assessing Children's Learning   110

For the Children   110

*Standard 1. Maps Use Lines, Color, and Other Symbols to Represent Reality
    and Are Used to Locate Oneself in Space   110*
Standard 2. Scale   112
Standard 3. Perspective   113

Just Pretend   113

Reflecting   114
Extending and Expanding to the Early Primary Grades   114
Documenting Children's Learning   114

9 Making and Keeping Friends   121

For the Teacher   122

What You'll Need to Know   122
*Key Concepts Based on CTB and Curriculum Standards
    for Social Studies   122*
Goals and Objectives   123
What You'll Need   123
The Home-School Connection   125
Evaluating and Assessing Children's Learning   125

For the Children   125

   Standard 1. Forming a Positive Sense of Self   125
   Standard 2. Recognizing Their Feelings and the Feelings of Others   127
   Standard 3. Learning How to Make and Keep Friends   128
   Standard 4. Resolving Conflicts Effectively   128
   Reflecting and Reaching Conclusions   129
   Extending and Expanding to the Early Primary Grades   130
   Documenting Children's Learning   131

10 Wants and Needs: Beginning Economic Concepts   135

For the Teacher   136

   What You'll Need to Know   136
   Key Concepts Based on Curriculum Standards
    for Social Studies   136
   Goals and Objectives   136
   What You'll Need   137
   The Home-School Connection   138
   Evaluating and Assessing Children's Learning   138

For the Children   139

   Standard 1. Identifying Wants, Needs, and Choices   139
   Standard 2. Learning About Production and Consumption   140
   Standard 3. Identifying Monetary and Barter Exchanges   141
   Standard 4. Learning About Work   142
   Reflecting   142
   Extending and Expanding to the Early Primary Grades   143
   Documenting Children's Learning   143

11 Living in a Democracy: From Choices to Voting   151

For the Teacher   152

   What You'll Need to Know   152
   Key Concepts Based on CTB Standards and Curriculum Standards
    for Social Studies   152
   Goals and Objectives   153
   What You'll Need   153
   The Home-School Connection   154
   Evaluating and Assessing Children's Learning   154

For the Children   155

   Standard 1. Children Are Capable of Making
    Choices   155
   Standard 2. What Voting Means   157
   Standard 3. Why People Vote   159
   Reflecting   160
   Extending and Expanding to the Early Primary Grades   159
   Documenting Children's Learning   160

12 Valuing Diversity 165

For the Teacher 166

  What You'll Need to Know 166
  Key Concepts Based on CTB Guidelines and Curriculum Standards
    for Social Studies 166
  Goals and Objectives 167
  What You'll Need 167
  The Home-School Connection 170
  Evaluating and Assessing Children's Learning 170

For the Children 170

  Standard 1. Valuing Cultural Diversity 170
  Standard 2. Valuing Others with Special Needs 172
  Standard 3. Valuing Gender Equality 173
  Reflecting and Reaching Conclusions 174
  Extending and Expanding to the Early Primary Grades 174
  Documenting Children's Learning 175

References 179

Resources 183

Index 185

PART ONE

Theory of Active Experiences

1

Experiences and Education
Putting Dewey's Theory Into Practice

All genuine education comes about through experience . . . but not all experiences are genuinely or equally educative.

John Dewey, 1938, p. 13

Active Experiences for Active Children—Social Studies guides teachers of 3- to 5-year-old children in planning and implementing meaningful learning experiences in the social studies for children in childcare settings, nursery schools, Head Start, and kindergartens. It is based on the concept that activities are simply that—isolated, one-shot occurrences. They begin and end quickly. They give children something to do but not something to learn.

Experiences continue. They may last a couple of hours or a day, but they could continue for a week, or even longer. Unlike fleeting, isolated activities, experiences are filled with learning. According to Dewey's philosophy of learning and teaching (Miettinen, 2000), experiences foster learning because they

- hold deep, personal meaning for children because they are grounded in children's firsthand experiences with their world, are initiated by the children, and are age appropriate;

- have meaning and integrity because the content stems from concepts key to a given discipline area;

- involve children in group work and interactions with teachers and other adults, promoting the skills and attitudes children need not only to perpetuate our democratic society, but also to continually improve that society;

- are covered with language;

- have continuity; one experience builds on another, forming a complete, coherent, whole, integrated curriculum for young children. Experiences also continue into children's homes and communities, serving not only to connect the curriculum, but to connect the early childhood setting to home and community as well; and

- provide time and the opportunity for children to reflect, think, and learn.

DEEP PERSONAL MEANING

Experiences are meaningful to young children because they engage children in firsthand learning in their here-and-now world, encourage them to initiate some of their own learning, and are age appropriate.

Firsthand Experience

This book involves children in firsthand experiences. Basing children's learning on content that can be experienced firsthand guarantees a measure of meaning. Children are not asked to gain knowledge secondhand, by listening to someone else tell them about a distant place or time. Rather, children are involved in touching, taking apart, tasting, and smelling things in their here-and-now world. By doing so, they are the ones who are receiving information directly and making sense of it.

Piaget's work fully documented that firsthand experiences are necessary if children are to learn, think, and construct knowledge (Piaget & Inhelder, 1969). When children actually handle objects in their environment, they gain knowledge of the physical properties of the world in which they live. As they experiment with a wide variety of objects and materials, they learn that some things are heavy, others light; some are rough or smooth, others sharp or rounded. These concepts cannot be taught through direct instruction, but can only be learned through firsthand experiences.

When children engage in firsthand experiences, their minds are as active as their bodies. By handling objects and observing things in their world, children begin to compare them. They classify and sequence objects and things, relating new information to their existing ideas of how the world works, fitting it into their schemes or ideas. When information doesn't fit their existing ideas, they change these or create new ones. As they do so, they are constructing their own knowledge and storing it as concepts, rules, or principles (Piaget & Inhelder, 1969).

Then, too, when children act on their environment, they are figuring out how to do things. They learn how to balance blocks, care for themselves and others, and become part of a democratic group. Through daily, firsthand experiences, children have the opportunity to confirm or change their ideas about how things work and what they can do with the things in their world. These initial, often incomplete and tentative, hypotheses and schemes about their world are the foundation on which all subsequent learning is built.

Initiative, Choices, and Decision Making

Experiences are designed so children can take the initiative and make choices and decisions. Children make choices from a variety of centers of interest. Once they have chosen a center in which to work, they make decisions about which materials from the center they will use. They may experiment and try something new, or they may simply decide to repeat an action, using the same materials over and over again.

Either way, children experience success because they select experiences that match their own interests, needs, and developmental level. In this way, children solve the problem of the match, or zone of proximal development, of which Vygotsky (1986) wrote. Vygotsky emphasized the zone of proximal development as the place where the child is close to developing strategies for problem solving or completing a task. The assistance of an expert, another child who knows how to do it or an adult, will push the child forward. When children are able to choose their own experiences, they are, as Bredekamp (1998) says, "identifying their own zone of proximal development." By doing so, they are ready for the questions or suggestions of experts who may be able to take children further along in their learning than they could go by themselves.

Children are asked to take the initiative throughout the day, not just during center time. Real problems that arise from living together give children the opportunity to take the initiative and make additional decisions and choices (Dewey, 1944). In one childcare setting, a group of 3-year-olds seemed unable to take part in clean-up time. After one particularly difficult and chaotic clean-up time, the teacher gathered the children around her and asked, "What happened?" One child replied, "We ran and threw things." Another said, "It was a mess." "Yes," the teacher agreed, "but what are we going to do about this? We must get our room cleaned so we can have lunch." Taking the initiative, one child said, "I'll put the dolls in the house"; another, "Casey and me put the blocks away." Others chimed in, and together they put the room back in order.

Children are also given the opportunity to experience the consequences of their choices. Teachers do not always protect them from making mistakes or from disappointments when they know the result of children's decision making will be less than positive (Dewey, 1944; McAfee & Leong, 2001).

Together children make decisions about their classroom environment.

By experiencing the consequences of their choices, children have a chance to reflect, to think about their actions, to determine which they would change, and to decide how or why the decision was or was not effective. In this way they develop the ability to think for themselves, which is so necessary if children are to become functioning citizens of a democratic society.

In one childcare center, Calan put the blocks away by himself as the other children listened to a story. When asked why he was not listening to the story with the other children, he replied, "It's logical consequences. You see, I didn't put the blocks away during clean-up time, so the logical consequence is I have to put them away now."

Dewey saw another purpose for asking children to take the initiative, to make choices and decisions (1944). He wanted teachers to use more "stuff" in schools. He asked teachers to include more raw materials and "stuff" so children could develop the ability to think. He believed that raw materials such as wood, clay, and paints—without any predetermined end or goal for their use—push children into thinking.

Given blocks, paper, and paint, children must figure out what to do with the materials, how to do it, and determine when their goals have been achieved. They are the ones who have to monitor their own thinking and doing. They are the ones who, when failing to achieve their goal, must decide how to change their actions or their plans. When they reach their goal, they are the ones who experience the joy of achievement and the satisfaction that comes from thinking and learning. Learning to take the initiative teaches children not to be dependent on others, but to develop an independence of thought necessary for them to become productive members of a democratic society (Seefeldt, 2004).

Age Appropriateness

Meaningful experiences are age appropriate. Experiences in this book challenge 3- to 5-year-old children, but at the same time are achievable. Children are not asked to repeat things they already know, or to achieve goals or objectives clearly beyond their capabilities, development, and maturation.

Experiences that are appropriate to children's developmental level enable children to experience success. Feeling successful, children come to think of themselves as learners who can and will achieve (Bredekamp & Copple, 1997). Research has demonstrated that children's success or failure during their early years predicts the course of later schooling (NRC, 2001). Research also shows that the more developmentally appropriate their early years the greater success children will experience when in the primary grades (Cassidy, Mims, & Rucker, 2003; Charlesworth, Hart, Burts, & DeWolf, 1993). Before selecting learning experiences, teachers should ask the following questions:

- Why is this worthwhile for this group of children or this individual child? For instance, why do 3-, 4-, or 5-year-old children need to learn about the rain forest? How would information about the rain forest relate to what children already know? How will they use this information?

- Why does this child or group need to learn it now? It may be important to learn about the rain forest, but is this something a child needs to know now?

- How efficient is it to teach this material to children of this age? There is no trick to teaching young children to do many things—learn the names of the days of the week or count to 100—however, will children learn these things more completely and efficiently when they are older?

CONTENT WITH INTEGRITY AND MEANING

Experiences have meaning and integrity in terms of content, more so than with simple activities. For example, what social studies content are children learning when they are asked to color in a picture of a Chinese child dressed in a traditional costume? Other than learning that school is filled with meaningless activities, or learning to follow the will of another, children learn nothing.

One teacher said she believed in firsthand experiences for children's learning. She decided to introduce a group of 3-year-old children to a standard from the field of history, that of change. To do so, she told children how years ago there were no zippers or Velcro and children had only buttons to fasten their clothing. After she talked, she gave each child a construction paper cut-out of a sweater and a bunch of buttons. She told the children to paste the buttons on the sweater. The question is, what did the children learn? To follow directions? To sit still and listen to a teacher?

Another teacher asked 3-year-olds to investigate how their clothes fastened. They listed zippers, Velcro, buttons, hooks, and belts as examples of fasteners. The teacher graphed how many of the children had pieces of clothing with zippers and so on. The next day she asked children to think about how their clothes would stay on if there were no Velcro, belts, and zippers. The children thought and thought and said, "We'd only have buttons, only buttons." The teacher then showed children antique clothing and accessories, including button-up shoes and a buttonhook, she had obtained from a local museum. The children handled the clothing, looking for how the clothing was closed. Some of the dresses had no fasteners at all. The shoes with the rows and rows of buttons fascinated children as they learned to use the buttonhook.

After the children explored the clothing over a number of days, the teacher read a book about children living during the Civil War. During the discussion that followed, the 3-year-olds determined that today's clothing was easier to get on and keep on, and it was too bad that long ago there were no zippers.

In the process, children reflected, predicted, posed questions, and found answers. They hypothesized about what life would be like without fasteners. They marveled over all the different ways people fastened their shoes. They discussed ideas together, and then graphed and sketched them. By doing so, the experience with fasteners had integrity. The content came from one of the history standards, and their firsthand experiences provided them with the opportunity to think, work together, learn, and problem solve.

Good teachers have always been concerned about fostering children's concept development (Sarnecka & Gelman, 2004). Concepts, the ingredients for thinking, are like mental filing cabinets in which related facts are connected and organized into an idea. Without a store of concepts, children are limited in understanding their world to dealing with isolated facts and bits of information.

For example, without a concept of jobs or occupations, humans would have to memorize the name of each and every profession or occupation they encounter because they could not conceptualize or categorize occupations into a singular idea or concept, such as everyone needs an occupation, job, or profession. With the ability to group things into categories, or to think in terms of concepts, we are freed from focusing on each isolated fact. With concepts, children have knowledge of how facts and pieces of information are related and interrelated. They understand something because they've organized the information into a concept; it has meaning to them. Today, experts from nearly every subject area have identified concepts key to their discipline in the form of standards. For example, the social studies standards are history, geography, economics, multiculturalism, civic participation, and democracy. These organized concepts give direction and guidance to planning curriculum for young children. In addition, the National Council for the Social Studies has organized the standards around 10 integrated themes, six of which are reflected in this book.

- **Culture**   The study of culture—the art, language, history, and geography of different people—takes place across the total curriculum. To become a citizen of today's global community, children must be exposed to the universals of human cultures everywhere. Chapter 3, Building Connections to Home and Community Through Active Experiences, and Chapter 12, Valuing Diversity, offer teachers guides to developing children's ideas of the things that unite all humans.

- **Time, Continuity, and Change**   In the context of their lives, children come to understand themselves in terms of the passage of time and develop the skills of the historian. This theme is reflected in Chapter 6, The Past Is Present: History for Young Children.

- **People, Places, and Environments**   Children learn to locate themselves in space, become familiar with landforms in their environment, and develop a beginning understanding of the human-environment interaction. Chapter 7, Earth: The Place We Live, and Chapter 8, Mapping for Young Children, present these ideas.

- **Individual Development and Identity**   Personal identity is shaped by one's culture, by groups, and by institutional influences. How people learn, what they believe, and how people meet their basic needs in the context of culture are themes within this topic. Chapter 9, Making and Keeping Friends, focuses on developing children's sense of self and extends to children learning to interact socially with others.

- **Individuals, Groups, and Institutions**   Institutions such as schools, families, government, agencies, and the courts play a role in people's lives. Children can develop beginning concepts of the role of institutions in their lives. Chapter 5 discusses different kinds of families. Chapter 7 includes the study of children's families, as well as institutions. Chapter 11, Living in a Democracy: From Choices to Voting, introduces children to the fact that within a democracy, individual rights are balanced with those of the group.

• **Production, Distribution, and Consumption**   Because people have wants that often exceed the resources available to them, a variety of ways have evolved to answer questions such as "What is to be produced?" and "How is production to be organized?" Chapter 10, Wants and Needs: Beginning Economic Concepts, is designed to enable young children to develop embryonic ideas of these concepts.

INVOLVING OTHERS

Interacting with the physical environment is not the only prerequisite for learning. Children must also interact with their peers, teachers, and other adults if they are to have true experiences. Both adults and peers are sources of information for children and serve as sounding boards against which children can test the accuracy of their thinking and knowledge (NRC, 2000). Therefore, all of the experiences in this book involve children in play, in group work and projects, and in interactions with teachers and other adults.

Play

Children are given the time and opportunity to play, especially in sociodramatic play that requires other children. Props relevant to the content are placed in the dramatic play areas and in the play yard to encourage children to reflect on and re-create their experiences. Both Vygotsky (1978) and Piaget (Piaget & Inhelder, 1969) believed this type of play led to symbolic thought. When children play "as if" they were the mother, baby, father, or teacher and "as if" a block were a scissors, they are thinking abstractly. Not only are they using objects to symbolize something not present, but they are convincing each other that the block is a scissors (Bodrova & Leong, 2003).

Other types of play—play with board games, organized circle games, building with blocks, outdoor play, play with puzzles and other materials—are also a part of the curriculum (Cooper & Dever, 2001; Levin, 2000). Each of these types of play gives children practice in observing, sorting, ordering, discriminating, classifying, and predicting.

Rough-and-tumble physical play is just as critical to concept development and learning (Perry, 2003). Research points out that children only learn concepts of in and out, up and down, and other directions by experiencing themselves climbing in and out, running up and down, or being high or low on the jungle gym (Piaget & Inhelder, 1969).

Group Work and Projects

Children are assigned to a small group to carry out a specific project. For example, teachers may ask two or three children to go to the school office to find all the machines that are used to communicate, or to be responsible for the plants or pets in the classroom.

Other kinds of small group work are arranged. Children may form some of these groups themselves, selecting one or two friends to join them in creating a mural or in doing some other task. Other groups may include children from another class or children of differing ages.

From time to time the entire group of children will meet together. Listening to stories, singing songs, making decisions about their classroom, sharing news, or listening to a visitor involves the entire community of children. These thoughtfully planned group meetings are valuable even for the youngest of children. First, they give children practice in following a common idea, arguing a point, listening to others' viewpoints, and forming their own opinions. More importantly, however, they build a sense of community (Box & Little, 2003; Dewey, 1944). By singing together; by listening to stories, poems, and rhymes together; and by sharing news and information, children feel a oneness with others that is critical to becoming a member of a democratic society.

The informal give-and-take that happens as children play with others, work in small groups, or meet together as a total group is important for several reasons. These naturally occurring interchanges challenge children to adjust their egocentric thought to assimilate and accommodate differing points of view. Doing so, they develop new ways of understanding the world in which they live. Then, if children are to get along at all when playing and working together as a group, they must consider the ideas, thinking, and wishes of others (Piaget & Inhelder, 1969). As children argue about where the blocks should be stacked, or how to represent the fire truck they saw on a walking field trip, they are gaining the skills involved in taking the perspective of others. Considering that others have views that may differ from one's own is critical for the perpetuation of democracy. The ability to take the perspective of others is necessary if children are to learn to give up some of their own individuality for the good of the group.

Interactions with Teachers and Other Adults

Dewey's idea (1938) that children's education takes place primarily through the process of sharing experiences includes an active role for the teacher and other adults. Arguing against traditional formal education in which a teacher lectures to passive students, he saw the role of the teacher in experiential learning as more demanding, calling for more intimate, complex interactions with children, rather than less guidance and involvement.

Today, it is recognized that children do not learn in isolation and that adult interaction in children's learning and development is not only valuable, but necessary (Bredekamp & Rosegrant, 1995). If children are to learn through experiences, then teachers and other adults must carefully structure their interactions with all children that are within what Vygotsky (1978) termed the "zone of proximal development." Bredekamp and Rosegrant (1995) describe the zone of proximal development as "teaching on the edge of children's knowledge" so children are challenged to new and higher levels of thinking and learning and are able to successfully achieve these.

COVERED WITH LANGUAGE

Language and experiences go together. You cannot have one without the other. Experiences demand listening, speaking, writing, and reading.

Experiences give children something in common to talk about. Probably every child in our country has been to a supermarket. However, when children go as a group for a specific purpose, they see the store differently. Because they share the same experience, they have a foundation for communicating with one another. From the common experience of going to a supermarket or some other place in the community or school, themes for sociodramatic play, murals, and other group projects emerge. These in turn give children still more to talk about and listen to.

Written language is necessary. Before taking a trip, children must write or dictate a letter to the store manager about the purpose of their trip. They also need to write or dictate a list of questions they'll ask the store manager, as well as a thank-you note after their visit. Following the visit, they can draw, paint, build, or write about their experiences.

Children consult and read books. Depending on children's needs, these could include reference books, picture dictionaries, picture books, and storybooks, both factual and fiction. Books are not just in the library area, but are found in the housekeeping area, near the blocks, or in the science and mathematics areas.

Learning requires physical, mental, and social activity.

CONTINUITY OF LEARNING

Because children's growth is continuous, their early educational experiences must also be continuous (Scully, Seefeldt, & Barbour, 2003). One experience builds on another. A thread of meaning runs through a number of experiences, forming a coherent, whole, continuous learning curriculum for young children.

Experiences can stem from every discipline. Some revolve around concepts key to mathematics; others arise from the biological and physical sciences, the earth sciences, music, dance and the visual arts, and the social studies. Each experience is chosen, however, because it builds on a previous one and leads to new experiences. Experiences are chosen not only because they are connected to other experiences, but also because they will enhance, deepen, and strengthen children's concepts, ideas, and perceptions of content.

Experiences continue over time. They are not one-shot occurrences that begin and end quickly. Nor are they units that begin on Monday and end on Friday. Experiences continue, each expanding and extending the other. Time is given so children can continue to expand and extend their ideas and work. They know as they leave school each day that when they return, there will be something for them to continue doing, learning, and experiencing.

Teachers in Reggio Emilia, Italy, understand the need for continuity of experiences. The video, *To Make a Portrait of a Lion* (Commune di Reggio Emilia, 1987), illustrates how children's interest in stone lions guarding one of the village squares led to a year-long study of lions. Children sat on the lions, drew them, looked at pictures of lions in books, visited museums to see other portrayals of lions, and learned where lions live.

When experiences are continuous, children have the time and opportunity to see relationships between facts, to develop ideas, to generalize, to extrapolate, and to make a tentative intuitive leap into new knowledge. This leap, from merely learning a fact to connecting one fact to another, is an essential step in the development of thinking (Bruner, 1966).

Continuity should be present across children's early childhood years. This means curriculum experiences should be coordinated and continuous from one school placement to another. Thus, *Active Experiences for Active Children—Social Studies* offers suggestions for extending and expanding experiences so they can form a complete whole as children progress from preschool to kindergarten and into the early primary grades.

Just as experiences serve to integrate the curriculum and connect children's thinking, so can they serve to unite home and school. This book demonstrates how to involve parents in children's learning. Each experience specifies a role for children's families so families will be active partners with teachers in the education of their children.

TIME TO REFLECT

Children are given time and the opportunity to reflect, to think about their experiences. Dewey (1938) maintained that only as children are able to reflect on an experience are they truly engaged in learning.

Reflection can take a number of forms (Miettinen, 2000). Children need the time and opportunity to pull away and be by themselves so they can reflect on what they are doing. At other times, children will be asked to reflect on their experiences by organizing their ideas, presenting them to others, applying their knowledge, communicating it to others, and evaluating their experiences.

Being able to pull away for a while and reflect on an experience is necessary. Young children in group care or educational settings, especially, need space, time, and freedom to be alone once in a while.

One kindergarten class built a large police car out of blocks. Over a month or so they added seats and a steering wheel, and one morning their teacher brought in some wires, a battery, and light bulbs. All the children tried, at one time or another during the morning, to attach the wires, light bulbs, and battery properly. Sasha sat alone at a table. She did absolutely nothing all morning except stare out the window or watch the children trying to make the lights on the police car work. Near the end of the morning, she left the table, walked to the police car, and with the help of the teacher and some children, showed them how to attach the wires, turning on the lights of the police car. The teacher, when asked why she let Sasha just sit all morning, replied, "Well, how would you expect children to think if we can't let them be alone to daydream?"

In addition to being alone and thinking, pulling away can also mean children will listen to tapes or CDs, view videos, or look at and read books by themselves. But it is perfectly acceptable to foster reflection by allowing and even encouraging children to daydream, sit and observe others, or play by themselves in a center.

Organizing

Children can organize their experiences in different ways. They might create a display to illustrate what they have learned. One kindergarten group studied rocks. With the teacher helping them, children grouped different types of rocks they found in their community, labeled them, and placed them on a table. The teacher added photographs of the children taken when they found different rocks and a title for the display.

Children in the childcare centers of Reggio Emilia are often asked to organize their ideas by making displays that document their experiences and what they have learned. One group organized their knowledge of dinosaurs by constructing a large dinosaur of boxes and found objects. In another class, children painted a large mural of their trip to a field of flowers.

Teachers can help children present their ideas through bar graphs or other types of graphs to organize an experience. For example, a kindergarten class tasted a variety of seeds and voted for their favorite one. The teacher then made a graph of their votes.

In contrast, an individual or a small group of children might make a presentation to the total group. Children could tell about their experiences, perhaps by showing pictures of the different birds they saw feeding at the window feeder or how they built a fire truck out of boxes. If children do not want to tell about their experience, they could dance, act, move, sing, or show others how they did something or what they learned.

Children can be asked to apply their knowledge. They might use their knowledge of numbers to plan snacks for the group, select a specific number of friends with whom to play a game, or count the days until their birthday.

Dewey believed that an experience is not complete until it has been communicated to another. That is why children are asked to draw, paint, or write about their experiences, communicating their ideas to others.

At times, children might be encouraged to communicate something they've imagined rather than experienced. Imagination is a form of thinking, and children enjoy drawing or painting an imaginary trip to the moon or illustrating an imaginative story or an imaginary ending to a favorite story.

Evaluating

Finally, children are asked to evaluate their own learning. Even 3-year-olds can be asked to think about the things they enjoyed doing during the day. In addition to thinking about the things that went well for them during the day, 4-year-olds can also be asked to think of the things they would change, as well as how they have grown and what they have learned. As 5-year-olds, children can pick out their best work to include in a portfolio, decide how completely they gained a skill, and rate themselves on how well they accomplished specific tasks. They can also be asked to tell about all the things they know now that they did not know at the beginning of the year, or when they were younger, and to tell what they want to learn next and how they could learn it.

Teachers take time to reflect on their work, as well as children's learning. Daily, they reflect on their program and the curriculum, asking themselves these questions:

- How far have I come in achieving my goals for myself and the children?

- What routines, interactions with the children, and experiences will I repeat tomorrow?

- Which things will I change?

Teachers also find ways to evaluate children's learning. They observe children informally as they work and play together, talk with them individually to find out what each child understands and what will challenge each, collect samples of work to include in portfolios, and use checklists to determine how children are progressing.

SUMMARY

Children learn from experiences because, through hands-on, minds-on activities, they are actively engaged in making sense of themselves in their world. Because experiences are embedded in children's here-and-now world, they are of interest to children. This interest motivates children to meet the challenges of the experiences and become successful learners.

Experiences continue. When children leave school for the day, they should always know there will be something for them to continue doing when they return. The fact that experiences are based on concepts key to a discipline not only gives them intellectual integrity, but offers children continuity of content. Because experiences are connected to children's homes and communities, there is a continuous thread of learning in children's lives.

By using language, working with others, and having the opportunity to reflect on their experiences, children are active participants in their classroom community. This participation prepares them to take their place as knowledgeable, active citizens of a democratic society.

2

Active Children—Active Environments

Any environment is a chance environment unless it has been deliberately arranged with reference to its educative effect.

John Dewey, 1944, p. 19

If active children are to learn through active experiences, then their environment must be carefully, thoughtfully, and deliberately arranged. Both indoor and outdoor spaces must be structured so children can

- engage in meaningful firsthand learning by taking the initiative and making choices and decisions;

- develop socially through working, playing, and interacting freely with others, both peers and adults;

- use language, talking, listening, writing, and reading in connection with their interactions with their physical world and socially with others;

- experience success as they gain new skills through interaction with their physical environment; and

- be alone so they can reflect on their experiences.

Beginning with the essentials—health, safety, inclusion, and beauty—teachers plan for children's meaningful learning experiences by structuring and deliberately arranging both the indoor and outdoor learning environments. Teachers not only deliberately arrange physical environments for active learning, but they also plan ways of interacting with children that foster and promote children's learning and development. According to Seefeldt (2002), "surrounded by beauty, children are motivated to create beauty themselves" (p. 97). Well-thought-out centers should be clean, ordered, and consist of:

- Growing things such as plants, flowers, fish, and insects.

- Natural things such as seashells, rocks, and twigs.

- Hanging things of the children's own creation.

- Works of art that are both child and adult inspired and created. The work of children's book illustrators may be introduced, with their books displayed throughout the room.

THE ESSENTIALS: HEALTH, SAFETY, INCLUSION, AND BEAUTY

Health and Safety

The indoor and outdoor learning environments must be set up with each child's health and safety in mind:

- Equipment must be checked for sharp edges, loose pieces that could cause accidents, or small parts that children might swallow or stuff in their ears.

- Equipment must be disinfected by daily washing with detergent in water, rinsing with clear water, wiping or spraying with a solution of two tablespoons chlorine bleach and one gallon of water, and sun or air drying.

- Rules for using each indoor or outdoor center must be carefully formulated, discussed at intervals with the children, and posted prominently as a reminder.

Planning for Inclusion

The physical environment can be arranged in ways that enable all children to participate actively and fully in all experiences. To permit use of a wheelchair, remove physical barriers, provide wider paths, and arrange work spaces and activity units to offer shelter from intrusion or interference (Loughlin & Suina, 1982). The careful use of space is an essential consideration for children with physical or visual needs.

Reducing the amount of visual stimulation in a given area aids children who are visually impaired. Teachers have found that they can add textures or raised patterns to the walls to enable visually impaired children to locate themselves in space. Others find that offering small shelving units, with a few materials on each shelf, is helpful.

Hearing-impaired children require more visual stimulation and less auditory distraction. Felt pads on tabletops, carpeted shelves and other work surfaces, as well as the clear display of all materials and equipment will be helpful (Seefeldt & Barbour, 1998).

Mitchell (2004) suggests that a teacher should consider the materials to be used for each activity and ensure that they will meet the needs of all children. For example, children with motor needs will profit from adding larger-sized brushes to the art area. Time is another important element. Children who have special needs may need additional time to participate actively with their classmates. Teachers may want to plan with flexibility in mind so that all children have time to complete their activities. To meet the needs of children with special needs, it is important to use visual, auditory, and tactile cues and to carefully label areas of the classroom where appropriate.

The physical environment is arranged to permit use of a wheelchair.

Beauty

Aesthetics and beauty must be considered. The childcare centers in Reggio Emilia, Italy, illustrate the wonder and beauty of environments created with aesthetics in mind. Stepping into a childcare center in Reggio, one knows immediately that the environment has been carefully arranged to simplify and order the children's world as well as surround them with beauty (Seefeldt, 2001).

Open rooms, filled with light and air, are simply and elegantly arranged. There is no clutter, but rather a clear, clean conceptualization of an environment specially arranged for active children who learn through active experiences.

Everywhere you look there is something beautiful to wonder over and ponder. Mirrors of all types are found throughout the center. Bits of mirrors and colored glass hang in front of windows to catch a sunbeam and bounce it back to children. Long horizontal mirrors are mounted near the floor so children can watch themselves as they build with blocks or play with others. In other places, square or triangular pieces of mirrors decorate the walls.

Plants and flowers are ever present throughout the center in classrooms, in lunchrooms and sleeping rooms, and in the bathrooms. Prints and posters of real works of art (Honigman & Bhavnagri, 1998), not cartoon characters, are hung at children's eye level in halls, bathrooms, classrooms, and lunchrooms. Children's artwork is mounted, framed, and displayed, serving not only to stimulate children's thoughts and permit them to reflect on past experiences, but also to inform others of children's work.

This emphasis on aesthetics in Reggio "reflects an appreciation of detail and sensitivity to design consistent with Italian cultural tradition of creative endeavors" (Mallory & New, 1994, p. 10). Nevertheless, children everywhere, not just in Italy, deserve to live and learn in environments that are aesthetically pleasing and visually appealing (Seefeldt & Barbour, 1998).

INDOOR SPACES

Organizing indoor spaces with centers of interest permits active children to engage in active experiences. Centers of interest are areas of the room that are clearly defined with either actual dividers or suggested boundaries. They contain materials and equipment organized to promote specific types of learning. The materials are carefully arranged so children can see the choices available and make decisions about which materials they will use and how.

Whether designed for 3-, 4-, or 5-year-old children, or an early primary classroom, each room will have specific centers of interest.

Art Centers

Through the visual arts, children are able to give expression to their ideas, imaginations, feelings, and emotions. "The arts play a critical role in the human need for self-expression, for sharing thoughts and ideas, and for challenging old ways of thinking" (Matlock & Hornstein, 2004, p. 14). This expression is necessary if children are to reflect on their experiences and document them. Each day, children should have a choice of whether to draw, paint, model, cut and paste, or construct something. Materials are arranged on tables or shelves that are easily accessible to children. Easels, a variety of brushes, and fresh, thick paints are available every day. At other times, areas of the floor, or a table or two, can also be used for painting. All types of drawing materials—crayons, marking pens, chalk, even pencils for 5-year-olds—are stored on open shelves for children's selection. A junk box, with every type of material imaginable, and a sewing box, equipped with threads, bits of fabric, buttons, and large blunt needles, are available. A separate area should be provided for clay and modeling materials.

Because the visual arts give children a way to organize, reflect, and present their ideas or emotions, art materials are chosen that enable children to do so. For example, a group of children took a walking field trip to a tall, narrow building near their center. When they returned, they found long strips of paper added to the painting and drawing areas. In another center, children took a walk to see the cherry and crab apple trees blooming in their neighborhood. The teacher then equipped the easels and painting tables with a variety of pink, lavender, and white paint and papers.

A center for woodworking gives children other opportunities to re-create their experiences. Through wood sculpture, children may learn the names of local trees; different leaves and seeds that each tree produces; the types and colors of wood; the softness or hardness of wood from various trees; and the names of artists who use wood in their artwork (Bisgaier & Samaras, 2004). A great deal of supervision and direct teaching in how to use woodworking tools, followed by practice and exploration using soft wood and the tools, is necessary before children can actually construct a boat, plane, house, or toy out of wood.

A place for children to construct three-dimensional objects should also be included. Children can use any material with which to work. Found objects—boxes, feathers, shells, sequins, paper, silk, and brocade scraps—are stored on open shelves in aesthetically pleasing ways, inviting children to choose what materials they will use.

Book and Library Centers

The library area is a place where books are arranged along with tables, chairs, or cushions to entice children to stay and read. It is more than a shelf of books and a table, however. It is a place located away from other distractions where children will find every type of book: poetry, stories, folktales, picture books, reference books and materials, even sections from the newspaper specifically designed for children, as well as children's newspapers and magazines.

All children should find themselves reflected in these books. Books depicting the lives of children with special needs, as well as children of diverse cultural, racial, and ethnic backgrounds, will be selected (Blaska & Lynch, 1998). Alma Flor Ada's *A Magical Encounter: Latino Children's Literature in the Classroom* (2003) is full of excellent ideas and bibliographies. J. J. Beaty's *Building Bridges with Multicultural Picture Books for Children 3–5* (1997) covers all cultures using a thematic approach. Books for the teachers and children about African Americans, American Indians, and people with special needs are in Chapter 12 on diversity, but may be found in all chapters.

Catalogs are fun to include. Children can use these as "wish books," or, if two or more of the same catalog are in the area, children will play games with them: "I'm looking at a toy. It's red and black, and children ride on it. Can you find it?"

Mounted pictures cut from magazines and depicting a topic the children are studying are fun for younger children to sort through and carry around with them. Books dictated or written by the children, or photo albums and stories written by the teacher, are other favorites. Some library areas also include a flannel board with cut-out stories for children to put into sequence or to use to retell a story by themselves or with a group of children.

Some books may be organized as a take-home library for the children so their learning experiences can continue outside of school. A simple checkout sheet with two markers attached can be mounted above the books. The children can place a check by their name with the red marker when they take a book out and a check with the black marker when they return it.

Books will also be displayed and arranged throughout the room. In one Head Start center, children observed a construction site and were fascinated with the trucks, cranes, and earthmoving equipment they saw. When they returned to the room, the teacher placed several books on trucks and construction vehicles in an open box next to the blocks. Children were seen consulting these as they created their own buildings.

In another classroom, teachers added Mother Goose and other nursery rhyme books in the housekeeping area. Children used these to read their babies to sleep.

Sociodramatic Play Areas

The primary sociodramatic play area is the housekeeping center, where children engage in playing house with others, enacting the roles they observe in their homes. From time to time, other sociodramatic play areas will be arranged so children can play store, gas station, business office, or post office, or act out some other theme.

Children of all ages find the housekeeping area continually appealing. This is the place where dramatic play flourishes, and here children find a way to link their home to their school. When playing house, children are free to feel big and in control when they take on the role of a parent, or weak and helpless when they play as if they were a baby.

A stove, a refrigerator, and table and chairs are essential pieces of furniture. Cartons, wooden crates, or even boxes can represent these items.

Props reflecting children's home life are found in the housekeeping area. Some may reflect their parents' work world—briefcases, hard hats, work boots, or tools representative of parents' work. Others, such as dishes, pots and pans, baby dolls representing all ethnic groups, cribs, baby bottles, full-length and hand mirrors, alarm clocks, microwaves, discarded cell phones, calculators, computers, and clothes, will reflect children's life at home.

Materials will be selected that encourage children to use written as well as spoken language, including notepads, calendars, discarded checkbooks, address books, and pencils, markers, and pens for children to write with as they play house. Reading materials found in a typical home, such as small manageable sections of the daily or Sunday newspaper, current magazines, phone books, and books, also have a place in the housekeeping area.

No two housekeeping centers will be exactly alike or equipped with the same materials because each center will contain props representing the culture of children's homes. In one kindergarten class, several children were immigrants from eastern Europe. Therefore, the teacher borrowed a pierogi press from one of the families so these children could play as if they were making pierogies.

From time to time, other areas for sociodramatic play are appropriate. When children visit their parents who work in offices, or visit the school's office, an area for office play is applicable. A table framed with cardboard walls becomes an office cubicle. Telephone receipt books, bookkeeping forms—anything that looks official and has space for writing—along with pencils, erasers, and markers of all kinds belong in the office. Children truly enjoy using staplers, pencil sharpeners, and other office tools, especially rubber stamps with stamp pads.

Based on children's experiences with their world, other dramatic play areas will be pertinant. For instance, if children have visited

- a post office, then a post office with envelopes, stamps, machines to weigh objects, and cubbyholes in which to sort mail would be created.

- a fast-food restaurant, then a restaurant with aprons, hats, trays, boxes for food, cups and bottles, a cash register, and pretend money would be added.

- a supermarket, then a store, complete with a cash register, money, all types of food containers, cans, boxes, bags to pack, old cash register receipts, and other materials would be arranged so children could reenact their visit to the supermarket, taking turns being shoppers, clerks, bakers, or shelf stockers.

Areas for Manipulatives

In the manipulative centers, teachers arrange age-appropriate puzzles, board games, matching and bingo games, pegs and pegboards, construction sets, small plastic or wooden blocks or tiles, Tinkertoys, Legos, and other materials. All these give children needed practice in observing, sorting, ordering, discriminating, classifying, and predicting.

A few sets of regular decks of cards and other materials, such as large beads and buttons, nuts and bolts, washers, seashells, and other objects, are nice additions for sorting, counting, and categorizing. Things for children to string—beads, bottle caps with holes in them, and shoestrings—are enjoyable items.

Board games, such as Cherry Tree, Chutes and Ladders, and all types of bingo games, are important. When playing these games, children learn to take turns, follow group rules, and most of all, consider the thoughts of others (Vygotsky, 1986).

Science Areas

A place is needed where children can actively experiment with and explore both the biological and physical sciences (in some cases, more than one place). The materials in science centers will promote activity on the part of the children. One teacher arranged a pitcher of water and small cups on a table next to small containers of instant coffee, tea leaves, dirt, sand, beans, sugar, and salt. She gave the children the problem, "Which things will dissolve in water and which ones will not?" A clipboard with a checklist for children to record their findings should be a part of the center.

Other science centers could be equipped with things to weigh, measure, and balance. Magnets, compasses, prisms, magnifying glasses, and different kinds of mirrors and colored cellophane also promote children's active explorations.

Machines to take apart—clocks, pencil sharpeners, instrument-panel boards (all of which have been safety proofed)—along with screwdrivers and wrenches fascinate children who are curious about how things work. One group of 5-year-olds worked for days taking apart an alarm clock and recording their actions in detailed drawings.

Children conduct experiments and organize their experiences.

Living things might be a part of the science area if they are well cared for and are not safety hazards for the children. An ant farm, created from a discarded large food jar, intrigues children, as does a butterfly farm or a worm garden.

Block Areas

Blocks and spaces in which to build are essential. Ideally, blocks should be stored on open shelves with a place for each type of block. Storing all rectangular blocks on the same shelf, for example, fosters children's ability to classify. Blocks can, however, be stored in wagons or storage bins with casters on the bottom.

A complete set of wooden unit blocks is the best investment a center or program can make. If these are unaffordable, blocks can be made from paper cartons.

Additional props for block play include toy traffic signs; sets of wooden or plastic farm, zoo, or domestic animals; and toy trucks, cars, airplanes, trains, and boats. These extend children's social studies concepts as well as represent their experiences. *The Block Book* (1996), edited by E. S. Hirsch, provides the teacher with connections to curricular areas such as science, mathematics, social development, art, literacy, and social studies. *Building Structures with Young Children* (2004) by Ingrid Chalufour and Karen Worth connects block-building with science through structured and unstructured explorations.

Water and Sand Areas

Children need areas where they can explore the properties of both water and sand and develop concepts of the surfaces of the world in which they live. Water is easy to provide. All that is needed are a low table; a small, plastic pan; some plastic cups and containers—spoons, funnels, plastic tubing—and a small amount of water. Sometimes teachers fill an old plastic wading pool and place it on a piece of plastic on the floor. If the room has sinks, children could play at these. If children tire of plain water, adding a bit of detergent enables the children to wash their hands, paint brushes, or doll clothes.

Sand, in a sand table, plastic tub, or old wading pool, can readily be available indoors. As with water play, children enjoy a variety of containers from which to pour and measure sand, or mold and shape sand into shapes and buildings. Water must be handy if children are to build with sand, however. Some teachers, objecting to sand indoors, find they can substitute rice, beans, or sawdust for indoor pouring and measuring.

Music/Movement Areas

According to Kemple, Batey, and Hartle (2004), teachers may not recognize the full value and potential of providing for children's musical development and may not understand the many ways musical involvement can enhance development and learning in other areas. The fact is, the teacher does not have to be a musician to promote music and movement in the classroom and enjoy simple yet meaningful music activities.

A part of the room, away from other activities, can be established as the music/movement center—a space in which children can listen to, as well as create, music and movement. Here, children listen to a CD or tape, operating the player by themselves. Or they play with whatever musical instruments they desire. A piano, an autoharp, a drum, a guitar, shakers, bells, and other rhythm instruments can be kept on hand. Children assume responsibilities by learning to handle and experiment with real musical instruments without damaging them. In addition to the intrinsic worth of music/movement exploration, young children seem to learn other content areas of the curriculum through music. Of Howard Gardner's (1993) eight intelligences, music seems to emerge first and involves the ability to hear, recognize, and remember patterns. Music also carries great cultural weight, and the exploration of music from many cultures provides the child with insights not gathered through any other form of learning.

Computer Stations

Several computers can be set up with age-appropriate programs that

- teach some skills more effectively than traditional and less expensive methods and materials.
- have the potential to help children develop higher-order thought skills like judging, evaluating, analyzing, or synthesizing information (Wright & Shade, 1994).
- present accurate information.
- do not emphasize war, violence, or discrimination against women or any racial/ethnic group.
- provide for more than one child to work with a program.

Quiet Spaces

Children need space to be alone or with one or two others. It may be a corner of the room, with a few pillows on the floor, a small nook in the library area, or a chair and table somewhere away from the other centers. Every room needs a space—wherever it is, or whatever it consists of—where children can be away from the group and can relax, calm themselves, and think.

Cooking Spaces

If space permits, a cooking program provides great benefits for children. Cooking brings celebrations to mind, good smells, the transformation of ingredients, sharing, language development, and builds family and cultural themes. However, the question of nutrition is of pressing national concern today. Of course, health and safety come first when a teacher considers how and where to conduct the program. *The Cooking Book: Fostering Young Children's Learning and Delight* by Laura Colker (2005) is a good resource for integrating all aspects of children's cooking into the curriculum.

OUTDOOR SPACES

Children need the exhilaration, challenge, and freedom inherent in outdoor play. Rough-and-tumble outdoor play gives children the opportunity to develop feelings of confidence, not only in themselves and their bodies, but also in others and their natural environment. Children with special physical needs find outdoor play of special value. Here they can strengthen large muscles. Depending on their needs, they can walk up and down hills, climb, and exercise small muscles by digging in the sand or playing in water.

Even though outdoor play is basically for large muscle physical development and exhilarating play, it also fosters children's autonomy and their ability to take the initiative. It also provides for additional learning experiences through increases in three areas:

1. **Sensory experiences.** Being out-of-doors offers new and varied sensory experiences (Stone & Glascott, 1998). Outside, there are different textures for children to experience, different weather conditions, and different surfaces to walk on and ride trikes over.

   Water and sand play can expand out-of-doors. On a hot and sunny day, children can play with water and hoses or run through a sprinkler. They can wash doll clothes and hang them in the sun to dry, or hold a car wash and wash all the trikes, wagons, and wheel toys. Adding a trickling water hose and plastic squirt bottles filled with water to the sand area lets children create large structures in the sandbox.

   Digging in the dirt is another sensory experience that can take place only out-of-doors. Many 3- to 5-year-olds enjoy digging just for the fun of it. However, it's more than fun. By digging in the earth, children are gaining sensory information about the nature of the surfaces of the earth, as well as concepts of heavy and light, soft and rough.

2. **Observation.** The natural world is filled with things for children to observe. Clouds, rain, sprouting seeds, falling leaves, birds, insects, shadows—all are experienced out-of-doors.

3. **Opportunities to cooperate with others, constructing large buildings and objects.** Of course children play cooperatively indoors, but being outside somehow fosters more expansive, and often long-term, cooperative efforts. Complex schemes for rearranging equipment, digging gardens, making cities in the sand, or building large structures develop and bloom out-of-doors.

PHYSICAL ACTIVITY

Space and a variety of equipment foster boisterous running, jumping, and climbing out-of-doors. Equipment that promotes social interactions, use of language, and cooperative play is rich with potential for children to form concepts of the physical properties of their world. Examples of this equipment include:

- Large wooden crates and boxes, boards with cleats, and large hollow blocks. The size of these materials demands that two or more children work together to use them for building.

- Climbing equipment that comes in several movable sections, such as a trestle unit, a climbing gate, or an A-frame unit, that can be arranged and rearranged to meet children's changing interests or needs.

- Cable tables of assorted sizes, tree trunks with sharp branches removed, and sturdy wooden barrels. These items give children the opportunity to use large muscles as well as work cooperatively with others.

- Balance beams. An old log, several logs placed end to end, a board placed on its side, or stepping stones, patio stones, or old tires placed in a series give children several different ways to balance themselves in space.

- A wide assortment and variety of balls of all sizes and weights.
- Things to push and pull. These give children a sense of control over their environment. Large wooden or cardboard boxes, planks, old tires, even small cable tables can be rolled to new locations, stacked to make a tower, or pushed around the yard.

OTHER OUTDOOR ACTIVITY

The out-of-doors is really an extension of the stimulating, well-arranged indoor learning environment. The added richness of the natural surroundings and open spaces enhances possibilities for learning experiences. Centers of interest set up indoors can also be arranged in varying forms out-of-doors.

Sociodramatic Play

Any kind of structure will do to stimulate sociodramatic play. It can be a playhouse, but more likely a wooden platform, a tepee of bamboo stalks, or a couple of boxes arranged with a blanket over them. These will motivate children to engage in housekeeping play. Adding a couple metal muffin tins, wooden spoons, pots and pans, plastic dishes, or a hat or two can allow dramatic play to flourish out-of-doors.

Wheel toys placed near the housekeeping center increase the complexity of dramatic play. Parents can leave for work on bikes or in wagons, deliveries can be made, or firefighters can come to rescue the "house" and the people in it.

Art

Any art activity can take place outside. From painting with water to painting on large brown paper strips hanging on a playground fence, children can enjoy painting out-of-doors.

Children can draw on the play yard's hard surfaces with large chunk chalk dipped in water. Their creations will wash away with the next rain. Or they can use crayons or markers on large paper spread on the yard or tables. Modeling with clay and other materials is fun to do outside, as is building with large boxes, found objects, and other materials.

Science

With nature surrounding them outdoors, children approach science with dynamic curiosity and vivid interest. Experiences with the biological as well as physical sciences are plentiful.

The life cycle of living things can be directly observed and recorded in photographs, drawings, and graphs. Watching birds, insects, and mammals fosters the concept of the variety of life on the earth. A few butterfly nets aid in the study of insects (Rivkin, 1995). Seeds and bulbs can be planted and cared for.

Experiences with simple machines are abundant outdoors. Wheeled toys can introduce the principle of the wheel; a seesaw, the lever. Moving heavy boxes or other equipment can demonstrate the use of simple machines, such as an inclined plane or a lever. The physical properties of light are easily introduced outdoors. A prism catches the sunlight, and water and bubbles show the refraction of light.

Music

When the teacher brings an autoharp or a ukulele outdoors, children can join in singing familiar songs. Sitting in the shade of a tree or gathering around a picnic bench adds variety to outdoor time. An astute teacher can also pick up children's natural running, skipping, and hopping rhythms by beating a drum or other instrument. The outdoors affords children the opportunity to move freely and to express their feelings and emotions, unlike organized games, which have a different objective.

Math

Counting, classifying, ordering, and other mathematical concepts become real outdoors. The smooth stones a child gathers, the acorns another collects, the sticks or cups in the sandbox, the number of children waiting to ride a new trike—all these give children something meaningful to count. Children also classify the stones, insects, seeds, and acorns they find, or place them in order from smallest to largest, heaviest to lightest.

Organized Games

Organized games that begin and end spontaneously, such as Ring Around the Rosy, Frog in the Middle, Did You Ever See a Lassie?, Punchinello, and others, are a part of outdoor play and experiences. This includes traditional games such as marbles and jacks (Casbergue & Kieff, 1998). The values of playing organized games are many. By playing a game together, children develop concepts of

- cooperating, learning to give up some of their individuality for the good of the group.

- sequencing, learning and remembering what to do next.

- structured language. The repetitive language found in organized games introduces children to concepts of grammar.

THE TEACHER'S ROLE

Without a concerned, interested, and knowledgeable adult, even the best-equipped indoor or outdoor spaces fall short of offering children meaningful experiences. Based on knowledge of children, of their experiences at home and in the community, it is the adult who

- selects, arranges, and changes the indoor and outdoor centers, making sure the spaces remain uncluttered, safe, inviting, and accessible to all children, including those with special needs.

- schedules large blocks of time during the morning and afternoon for free play both indoors and out.

- provides a background of meaningful experiences with people, places, and things so children will have ideas—including the imaginary—feelings, and emotions to express through play.

Most of all, however, it is the teacher who interacts with children in ways that clarify, extend, and expand their knowledge and skills.

- Teachers observe and supervise children as they play. Observations can focus on the total group of children or on individuals. The progress children are making, the skills they are gaining, and the things they still need to learn can be noted. When needed, teachers step in—setting limits, clarifying rules, removing broken toys or objects, and supporting children in their attempts to learn new concepts, skills, and attitudes.

- Teachers enter into joint activities with children, working collaboratively with them on a problem or task, such as building a block structure, a rabbit hutch, or another specific item.

- Teachers extend children's play by entering into the play scene. A teacher of 3-year-olds subtly encouraged children who were playing shoe store by saying things like, "Where can I pay for my shoes?" and "This would be a good place to display shoes." These suggestions led children to organize and extend their play.

- Teachers use language to promote children's learning, naming things in the children's environment and giving information: "That sign says stop. When we see it, we stop and look both ways before crossing the street."

- Teachers ask a variety of questions that lead children to new learning: "Let's count the acorns; how many do you have?" "What colors are you going to use in your painting?" "Is your suitcase light or heavy?" "Where do I buy my ticket?"

- Teachers offer assistance to help a child solve a problem or achieve the next level of functioning: "Here, I'll hold this piece while you attach this part."

- Teachers plan and help children select activities that are appropriate for individual children's development and background of experiences.

- Teachers set expectations for classroom behaviors that are consistent with children's emerging cognitive and social capabilities (Berk & Winsler, 1995).

- Teachers demonstrate how to do something, supporting children as they try.

- Teachers give specific directions and information.

- Teachers seriously enter into conversations about children's work, focusing on the children, their work, and their ideas. Lilian Katz (1993) observed that teachers often seem reluctant to engage children in meaningful conversations and focus more on giving positive feedback—"You did that well," "Very good"—rather than talking about content, relationships, or even what the child is doing.

- Teachers carefully structure their interactions with children that are within what Vygotsky (1978) termed the "zone of proximal development."

- Teachers ensure that all children are able to take part in centers both indoors and outdoors.

SUMMARY

Active children need indoor and outdoor spaces that are specifically designed to foster active experiences. Planning indoor and outdoor environments begins with making certain the spaces are healthy, safe, beautiful, and accessible to children with special needs.

Indoor spaces are arranged with centers of interests. Centers organize children's environment, let them see the choices available to them, and give them the means to work and play cooperatively with others. The arrangement of outdoor spaces is equally as important if active children are to learn through active experiences. Not only can children experience large muscle play and activity outdoors, but just being outside enhances children's sensory experiences and their opportunities to observe their world and enter into cooperative play with others.

As Dewey (1938) suggested, the role of the teacher is more complex and more intimate when children are actively engaged in experiential learning. Teachers schedule large blocks of time for children's indoor and outdoor activities, and actively teach, guide, and interact with children.

3

Building Connections to Home and Community Through Active Experiences

These are the two great things in breaking down isolation, in getting connection—to have the child come to school with all the experience he has got outside the school, and to leave it with something to be immediately used in his everyday life.
John Dewey, 1900, p. 73

John Dewey believed that the classroom was a community, a place where young children learned how to function together to solve shared problems. However he also believed that schools could not function "when separated from the interest of home and community" (Dewey, 1944, p. 86). Dewey suggested that the school be viewed as part of the larger whole of social life. He depicted the school at the center with two arrows representing the free interplay of influences, materials, and ideas between the home life and that of the school. Similarly, he related the school to the natural environment around the school building, the wider country, and the business life of the community. The work of Piaget (Youniss & Damon, 1992) and Vygotsky (Berk & Winsler, 1995) confirms the importance of building connections to home and community through active experiences. According to Piaget, "culture acquiring" children construct knowledge about themselves and others within their culture or social world by interacting with other children and adults in school and beyond the school (Youniss & Damon, 1992). Vygotsky (1978) saw children learning to think and behave in ways that reflect their community's culture by mastering challenging tasks in collaboration with more knowledgeable members of their society.

In his ecological approach, Bronfenbrenner (1979) placed the developing child in the center of a series of interlocking settings. Home, school, and the neighborhood serve as the immediate basis for child development and learning. Just as active children derive meaning from their experiences in the classroom, that meaning is extended and broadened when teachers recognize the family as a resource for deep and personally meaningful learning experiences.

Thus, the immediate environment of the school and community serves as a laboratory or workshop for children to discover the world around them and the people and things that populate that world. Without these active experiences, children lack the raw material to construct learnings in the classroom that have meaning and integrity. Children are cheated when teachers provide pictures of birds, insects, and trees and expect children to form concepts from these instead of observing them in the world outside the school.

Ms. Green, a teacher of 4-year-olds, had attended some summer workshops and became convinced that it was necessary for her to build connections with the home and community through excursions into the wider community. Using her experience from the workshop, and the help of her colleagues, she formulated the following criteria for experiences with integrity and meaning:

- There is a continuity of experience as one builds upon another. Ms. Green had some experience with the policy of her school to take a field trip each week to a different place, and realized that the children were having a series of isolated experiences that were soon forgotten. Instead, to build experiences around one theme would help children construct knowledge in depth and to generalize it to other areas.

- Each experience is worth the child's and teacher's time and effort. A trip to the history museum had been long and exhausting. The exhibits had been placed too high for most children to see or touch. Worse, the docent was not used to young children and lectured them as she did secondary students. The children whined, fidgeted, and started poking and fighting with one another. Later, when asked what they remembered about the trip, the children talked only about the drinking fountains.

- Advance organizers such as KWL charts should be provided for the children. On the chart they can identify what they know, what they would like to find out, and what they actually learned. The chart may also be extended to include things they would still like to learn. Children need opportunities to discuss, read about, and role-play the excursion in advance.

- Children should have time to reflect upon and follow-up on experiences with plans and projects that enhance their learning.

- A planned experience should either be an outgrowth of children's deep interests or meet a specific need for the children in learning subject matter content. One of Ms. Green's colleagues was teaching her class about Irish dancing and cooking. While the children seemed to be having fun, Ms. Green believed that they were not developmentally ready to learn about a different country, nor did these activities have personal meaning to them.

- Flexibility is essential. While most outside experiences are well planned in advance, sometimes teachers can capitalize on incidental learnings, such as when children hear construction noises outside or spot a nest of baby birds.

OUT INTO THE SCHOOL

Now, where can the teacher and children find the active experiences that build connections to home and community and take them outside the classroom walls?

Whether in a kindergarten or a Head Start program in a large elementary school, a childcare center, or a small cooperative nursery school, there are many meaningful ways to utilize the immediate environment of the building itself and the grounds that surround it. One of the best places to begin building experiences about others in the children's world is to learn about the people in the children's most immediate environment. As with field trips into the neighborhood (or larger community for older children), teachers will want to become familiar with the people that contribute to making their school run, with the building, and with the immediate grounds. The following are examples of authentic and active experiences close to the classroom.

Persons in the Immediate Environment

Children who are in an elementary school setting can meet with the principal, a secretary, the nurse, a custodian, an office worker, the persons who pick up the garbage, the cook, and the letter carrier. The teacher might assist the children in preparing a list of questions to ask by getting them to think about how many people work in the school, who they are, and what they do. Children in one Head Start center wanted to know if the director was a mommy, what her favorite colors were, whether she had a dog or a cat, what her home or car was like, and finally, what she did all day. The teacher might want to construct a T-chart to record the questions and answers. It should look like this:

**Head Start Childrens' T-Chart
About the Director**

Questions	Answers
Does she have a dog or cat?	Yes, a dog

Inside the School Building

There are many active experiences for children when they take a walk around the school building. If the children have expressed an interest in shapes, colors, and textures, the teachers will ask them to note these as they explore the inside of the school. Directions and locations outside of the classroom can be emphasized. While terms such as *left* and *right* are not yet clear to them, young children are curious about what direction they should take to get to the big kitchen.

Outside in the Natural Environment

The immediate outdoor environment of the school can provide children with a rich laboratory for studying nature and their physical world. They should be encouraged to think of all the things they can observe outside and prepare to observe closely. Depending on the children's interests and classroom themes, they may gather data on flowers, trees, small animals, weather, sounds, and the seasons.

The child gathers data on flowers and plants them for beauty.

OUT INTO THE NEIGHBORHOOD AND COMMUNITY

Ms. Smith, a teacher of 3-year-olds in a childcare center, had heard how wonderful the regional park was. Yes, it was a 45-minute trip, but it would be worth it for the children to play on the wonderful equipment and talk to the rangers.

She planned to entertain them on the bus with finger plays and songs, and the assisting parents would enjoy it, too. It started well. Everyone was enjoying themselves and began singing "The Wheels on the Bus." That is, until several children started vomiting. Things went downhill from there. Children whined. The adults, exhausted from trying to comfort the children, became cross. On the return trip, everyone was anxious to see the familiar grounds of the center.

What went wrong here? First, was the trip meaningful, or was it a waste of valuable time and resources? Ms. Smith thought hard about these questions. She quickly understood that her 3-year-olds do not care about the wonderful equipment at the regional park, but love the equipment in their own playground, where they can also observe the plants in the sidewalk and the neighbors' yards. She realized that she had made an unwise decision. This long trip was not appropriate for the developmental level of the children in her classroom, although it could have been an excellent experience for older children.

In planning for meaningful experiences for children, teachers prepare the children, but they also prepare themselves. The purpose of a trip is to provide children with firsthand experiences, based on their interests, that they would be unable to have in the classroom, in school, or on the immediate grounds. In fact, the first step for the teacher might be to decide if the purpose could be accomplished another way. Do the children need to go to a museum, or would it be possible to bring artists or craftspeople into the school? If school visits are not possible, the teacher decides on the goals and then plans for experiences prior to, during, and after the trip.

Teachers will want to become familiar with the community and its resources prior to planning any trip. Unforeseen difficulties can be avoided if teachers preview the site, talk with the people at the places they wish to visit (such as the supermarket), and familiarize the staffs with the interests and needs of the children. Some sites such as museums, large supermarket chains, and libraries have prepared tours and materials for children; however, these items need to be appropriate for very young children. Teachers should shorten and modify an experience when necessary.

Teachers will also want to consider the integrative power of a field trip (Seefeldt, 2001). How will the trip facilitate growth in the language arts, mathematics, the use of books, writing, the arts, and social skills? As teachers prepare the children, they will emphasize active experiences in all of these areas.

Each active experience will involve learning new vocabulary words and investigating the site through informational books and fiction. Children will want to draw pictures and dictate stories about what they have done. They will re-create and reinvent their learnings through dramatic play inside and outside the classroom. Social skills develop as children experience new people and places and acquire behaviors to suit the situation.

BASIC GUIDELINES FOR MEANINGFUL FIELD EXPERIENCES

1. Keep the experience simple for very young children, and increase the complexity as it is developmentally appropriate. For example, very young children will profit from writing (pictorially and with the teacher's help) a letter or card to a friend or family member and walking to the mailbox to mail it.

2. Consider the mode of transportation. Walking is best for most children, yet some field trips necessitate bus or public transportation. In fact, when learning about transportation, a trip on the subway is an authentic and active experience.

3. If the classroom is inclusive, consider all aspects of the field experience. Pathways and sites must be barrier free and experiences must be open-ended so that all children profit from the field trip. Small group excursions provide a better opportunity for all learners to profit.

4. Introduce the field experience through discussions, pictures, mapping, reading about it, and art experiences. For example, if the children are to visit the produce department of the supermarket, they can cut, taste, and compare vegetables and fruit; cut pictures from magazines and make a collage; read about the nutritional value of various types of produce; and even vote on their preferences. Small group work in areas of particular interest should be encouraged.

5. Organize play around the places to be visited. The creative dramatic center and the block area can become a bakery, pet store, fire station, or construction site. The teacher will introduce additional props as necessary.

6. Prepare the children to observe closely and gather data during the field trip. Their observations will be used as the basis for many activities in the days and weeks to follow. For example, children may have been to the bakery many times with their parents, yet not paid close attention to the smells, variety of goods, and packaging of the purchases. They will probably get to see more on a planned trip, such as the stoves, the large sacks of ingredients, and the bakers

---

SOME SAFETY TIPS FOR FIELD EXPERIENCES

- Obtain parental permission for children to participate in the excursion.
- Check the environment ahead of time, both inside and out, for any hazards.
- Be sure all teachers and staff members are trained in first aid and CPR. Include at least one person with such training on the trip.
- Take a first-aid kit on the excursion.
- Take an up-to-date list of emergency phone numbers for each child.
- Check medical forms for children's allergies (including reactions to wasp and bee stings and foods) before food-tasting or outdoor experiences.
- Always walk on the left, facing traffic.
- Be sure that children understand that small wild animals are for observation and not handling.
- When utilizing transportation, make sure the children know, have practiced, and will follow the rules.
- Consider adult/child ratios. Include no more than three or four children on a field trip for each adult present and fewer if the trip requires complex arrangements for transportation.
- Remember that small group excursions may be best for all learners.
- Be sure the field trip site meets guidelines for children who are developmentally different.

and their uniforms. Questions originating from older children may be compiled on sheets to remind them of the experiences they wished to have.

7. Give children plenty of opportunities to reflect on their experiences. Allow time and materials for follow-up plans and projects. Isolated experiences are easily forgotten. Learnings from field trips are part of an integrated curriculum.

8. Welcome parents during any phase of the planning, implementation, or follow-up. Opportunities for parent participation should accommodate parents' schedules. Parents need not come to the school or field experience. There are many ways they can enhance their children's experiences in the home if they are informed of the teachers' plans and activities. Newsletters (translated for non-English speakers) help parents to feel part of the experience.

BUILDING CONNECTIONS WITH THE NEIGHBORHOOD AND COMMUNITY

For Democracy

Living in a democracy requires that young children begin the process of building connections to their immediate social group (their peers in the classroom), their neighborhood, and the broader community. Young children need to understand that they have responsibilities to fulfill in order to make their communities function. According to Dewey (1944), "A curriculum which acknowledges the social responsibilities of education must present situations where problems are relevant to the problems of living together, and where observation and information are calculated to develop social insight and interest" (p. 192).

While the classroom serves as a setting for making rules, resolving conflicts, expressing opinions, and making choices, Dewey believed that children need to see that

Learning to value the environment is a priority for today's children.

work, participation, and caring are what make a community possible. According to Swick (1997), "Communities offer multiple opportunities to extend and enrich children's conceptions of work. Learning to take care of the environment is a priority for today's children and an inviting place to connect work and human functioning" (p. 39).

Adopting a stream or a playground gives children a sense of responsibility and participation in society through real-life experiences. In our throwaway culture, young children can learn the habits of recycling—to reduce the amount of materials they waste and consume and to reuse whatever possible, such as using computer paper for other projects.

Additional ways to introduce children to community responsibility and caring include visits to a veterinary clinic, carefully facilitated intergenerational contacts, and opportunities for them to mentor and interact with classmates who are developmentally different.

Mr. Lopez, for example, noticed that the 5-year-olds he taught were treating classroom animals carelessly. He decided to plan several trips to the local veterinarian to foster empathy and understanding in the children. He believed that in the process of learning how to care properly for a small animal, the children would be introduced to a specific form of responsibility and caring. They would believe that they were doing valuable work and feel valued for it. He noticed improvement at the outset, and by the end of the visits, children were volunteering to care for the classroom animals and setting careful rules.

In carefully planned intergenerational programs, children and elders interact with one another, reestablishing the relationships of caring and continuity of life that have been broken by physical and social distance. The teacher will want to plan programs and contacts carefully since children tend to hold negative stereotypes about the elderly and in some instances fear such contacts. With this in mind, it would be unwise to take children to nursing homes where elders have symptoms of senility and infirmity.

Seefeldt (2001) suggests that when children are exposed to elders who are healthy, happy, active, and fulfilled, they can share the love of an older person: "Intergenerational programs in the school can provide a way for children and elders to enjoy one another's company, to learn from one another, to share feelings of affection, and to provide children with a concrete example of life's continuity" (p. 226).

Democracy recognizes the necessity of diverse capabilities within a community of learners. Inclusive early childhood classrooms afford all learners the opportunity to value the capabilities of all children, and to extend this experiential learning beyond the classroom to the neighborhood and community. Mallory (1998) suggests that children may serve as "peer advocates" who can help to identify the capabilities of classmates with special needs and who can offer suggestions for ways to accommodate their classmates' needs: "Suggestions regarding the placement of furniture and materials, the assignment of classroom responsibilities, when to offer assistance, and how to adjust planned activities to make them accessible to all children are examples of ways in which young children can be advocates for their peers with disabilities" (p. 229). To the extent that classroom experiences promote more opportunities for children with disabilities to be seen like everybody else and not as members of an "out group" who are "not like me," such experiences may promote the development of more positive attitudes toward classmates with disabilities (Diamond & Stacey, 2003). All children feel rewarded when inclusive classrooms function optimally, and the experiential learnings are generalized from the classroom community to the neighborhood and larger community. As mentioned earlier, the teacher will give special consideration to community trips when the classroom is truly inclusive.

For Diversity

According to Dewey (1944), "Every expansive era in the history of mankind has coincided with the operation of factors which have tended to eliminate distance between peoples and classes previously hemmed off from one another" (p. 86). The democratic classroom envisioned by Dewey would be ethnically diverse, yet Dewey might be surprised at the variety of cultures represented in many of today's schools for young children.

This diversity poses both great opportunities and great challenges. Bredekamp and Copple (1997) believe that it is the responsibility of the teacher to "bring each child's home culture and language into the shared culture of the school so that children feel accepted and gain a sense of belonging" (p. 124). Further, the teacher will ensure that the contributions of each child's family and cultural group are recognized and valued by others.

New (1998) calls on teachers in the field of early childhood education to accept both the responsibility and the potential to co-construct, with the help of the children and their families, a curriculum that rejects prejudice and engages children in critical thinking about diversity and constructive conflict when necessary. To accomplish these ends, teachers will examine their own attitudes as well as their background of information on the cultures of the children they work with each day, and other cultures that they may want to introduce into the curriculum.

Many authentic and active experiences may occur directly in the classroom as teachers capitalize upon the cultures represented and identify resources for learning about others. Some of these include making charts of the different nationalities represented in the classroom, discussing the customs of different families, and participating in these customs. Derman-Sparks (2003) suggests that quality markers for a multicultural/antibias curriculum include incorporating children's daily life experiences into curriculum, using parents' or family caregivers' knowledge about their home cultures to tailor curriculum, incorporating diversity and justice issues, using a variety of strategies to involve parents actively and regularly in the program, and encouraging children's development of critical thinking and tools for resisting prejudice and unfair behaviors.

Visitors

Visitors from other cultures serve as effective resource people if the teacher prepares carefully for their visits. Parents and other family members are most immediate in a child's life and help to bridge the cultural gap between home and school when they arrive to share a story or a game, or to speak to the children in another language. These experiences should be authentic and should serve to emphasize the commonalities more than the differences between people.

Books

Children's literature offers young children another way to understand and build community with those of different cultures. Folktales and more recent children's books that avoid stereotypes and the trivial differences between cultures should be available on a regular basis. Each active experience chapter in this book has books for teachers and for children that foster that goal.

Trips to the Community

Active experiences in ethnic neighborhoods immerse children in the sights and smells of a culture. At the same time children observe different types of stores and restaurants, signs in a different language, and buildings with architectural differences, they will also observe the similarities between peoples and their needs, learning how to collect data on what is similar and what is unique about themselves and others.

Libraries

Most children's librarians have set programs for young children, but they are anxious to accommodate the needs of particular groups. They also can provide a larger selection of children's books on any particular topic area. When asked to plan a multicultural program, one children's librarian read a picture book about a different country on each of four successive weeks. Each book was allowed to go back to the classroom so that the children might examine the pictures more closely and reread the story. On the fifth week, she asked the children to do the following with each book:

- Make yourself the main character. How would the story change? Why? How would it remain the same?

- Imagine one of the book's characters was at your house or in your neighborhood. Would the character be happy and comfortable? Why? Why not?

- Decide which character you would want as your friend. Why?

- Make a list of how the characters are like you and how they are different.

In addition to storybooks, children's rooms in public libraries have many nonfiction books that are appropriate for young children, as well as a variety of reference materials for research purposes. With the drop in funding for libraries, some of the large book chains have taken over "storytime" for children. While some of these programs can be quite good, the teacher should verify the potential quality of the experience in terms of depth and sensitivity to culture.

Museums

Children's museums hold additional resources beyond the school. These are especially important when young children do not live in proximity to neighborhoods where they can have firsthand experiences with the language and customs of various cultures. Historical societies and embassies also offer children concrete experiences with artifacts from other lands. Increasingly, such nonschool settings are providing programs for young children that supplement the curriculum of the school.

Children's museums provide hands-on experiences for young children that are both aesthetic and cultural. The Capital Children's Museum in Washington, DC, allowed children to "visit" Mexico by providing an authentic series of rooms where children may enter the houses, wear the clothing, cook hot chocolate and tacos, and make candles. Each center has a trained facilitator, and the museum provides follow-up suggestions for teachers.

Recently, the National Gallery of Art in Washington, DC, held an exhibit of the works of Alexander Calder. The exhibit featured a children's guide, which might serve as an example for excursions with children to an exhibit that would be of vital interest to them. The children's guide emphasized six important concepts that children can understand: color, movement, balance, line, shape, and size. The guide stated that while "many of the objects in this exhibition may be in motion or look as if they would move if touched, please do not touch" (National Gallery of Art, 1998).

Yet the guide posed questions that would keep children involved in an investigation of Calder's mobiles and stabiles. Since Calder liked to draw with a single, nonstop line, children were challenged to find a drawing, follow the line with their eyes, and identify where the line started and stopped. Similarly, children discovered the colors Calder used most often. They were asked to speculate why Calder chose to work with only a few colors.

At the Kreeger Museum in Washington, DC (2004), an experienced docent led the children in an interactive tour through a series of paintings emphasizing the theme of nature. By the end of the tour, children could articulate the very different ways painters could depict nature.

As in the previous example, teachers can create guides for children that will involve them in beautiful works of art and architecture without the children actually having to touch them. By posing leading questions, teachers provide children with authentic active experiences. Of course, the group should be prepared for an excursion to the museum, and many materials should be available in the classroom for follow-up activities related to aesthetics, just as music should be played and discussed prior to a short children's concert or dance performance.

The Home-School Connection

The family has long been considered the child's first and foremost teacher and possibly the child's primary community for learning (Bredekamp & Copple, 1997; Goleman, 1995). According to Swick and Freeman (2004), when children have ongoing, loving relations with family members and other primary caregivers, they are likely to see the world as a good and nurturing place. Teachers can utilize the family as a resource for children's learning both in the school and in the home. Interactions with family members serve to inform young children of their role in society (Seefeldt, 2004). Then, too, there is an increased research base on the benefits of family involvement to the child even if the extent of that involvement is small (Grolnick & Slowiaczek, 1994; Marcon, 1992; Stevenson & Baker, 1987).

Teachers and parents may face some challenges in working together. According to Powell (1989), early childhood educators increasingly service families characterized by single-parent households, cultural diversity and ethnic minority status, dual-worker or dual-career lifestyles, blended family arrangements, economic pressures, and geographic mobility. The new demographics of family structure call into question the viability of existing approaches to relations between families and early childhood programs.

Teachers' conceptions of working with parents may be based upon idealized images of the middle-class nuclear family. Yet, diverse families bring strengths to the early childhood program that secondary experiences could not provide. In fact, through interactions, children, parents, and teachers come to know each other as people. Everyday life incidents cement a genuine respect and tolerance for ethnic/cultural diversity and varying family structures. Involving parents as active partners in the classroom provides both parent and teacher with firsthand information about the expectations of the home and the school. Bredekamp (2003) challenges teachers to make a commitment to resolve contradictions without choosing between the values of the families and the school. Contradictions enhance the need for reflection and communication.

Classrooms work best, and children learn more, when families are involved. Teachers may employ the following multiple approaches:

- Interactive conferences in which teachers provide parents with samples of children's work and invite parents to share their observations about their children's learnings and their suggestions for classroom and community experiences based on their children's interests.

- Use of informal contacts. Busy families enjoy a brief chat before school, telephone calls, informal notes, and bulletin boards that inform them of plans and programs and invite them to participate in a variety of ways.

- Somewhat more formal contacts through the provision of a Parents' Corner or Family Room where parents may interact around learning materials and other activities of interest to the family. Often these include a lending library with toys as well as picture and reference books.

- Regular newsletters (translated into the languages of the families) explaining the goals for the week, why certain activities were planned, and how parents can support the lessons at home. Other items to include in newsletters are special events at school, poems and songs that children have enjoyed, special television programs that parents and children might watch together, and special events for children and families occurring in the community.

- An open-door policy for parent observation and participation. If parents are unable to work regularly as paid or unpaid volunteers, they may make or send materials for special projects in the classroom, help on field trips, or come to school when their schedules permit.

- Selection of active experiences for children that can be documented. Children will have products such as drawings, pottery, or stories to communicate to busy parents what they are doing in school.

Parents support the social studies by the interactions they have with their children at home. Children's daily activities with their families serve to inform them of their role in society. Family routines, traditions, and stories build continuity between past and present. As children learn about their family history, examine old photo albums, and look at mementos of important family events, they are learning cultural and social values.

Schools may use the child's family as the basis for active experiences. To gain knowledge of oneself in a social sense involves learning one's name, ethnic background, type of family, family occupations, and where one lives. All of these things originate in the informal learnings of the home. Children may be asked to interview family members about changes that have occurred over the years, lifestyles of the past, where the family has lived, and types of jobs family members have held.

Additionally, even if family members cannot volunteer in the classroom on a regular basis, they can share their talents, occupations, hobbies, customs, and traditions with the class or school community.

SUMMARY

Building and maintaining connections with home and community provides benefits to all. Young children need active experiences consistent with their participation in a democratic society, their valuing of diversity, and their appreciation of beauty. These experiences require careful planning by teachers, who are rewarded by observing children's authentic learning, as one experience builds upon another to create an integrated whole. As the family is recognized as a valuable resource for learning, parents and teachers feel mutually supported and learn to understand and value each other. All this is consistent with a strong emphasis on the social studies in the curriculum for young children.

4

Experiences and Social Studies Content

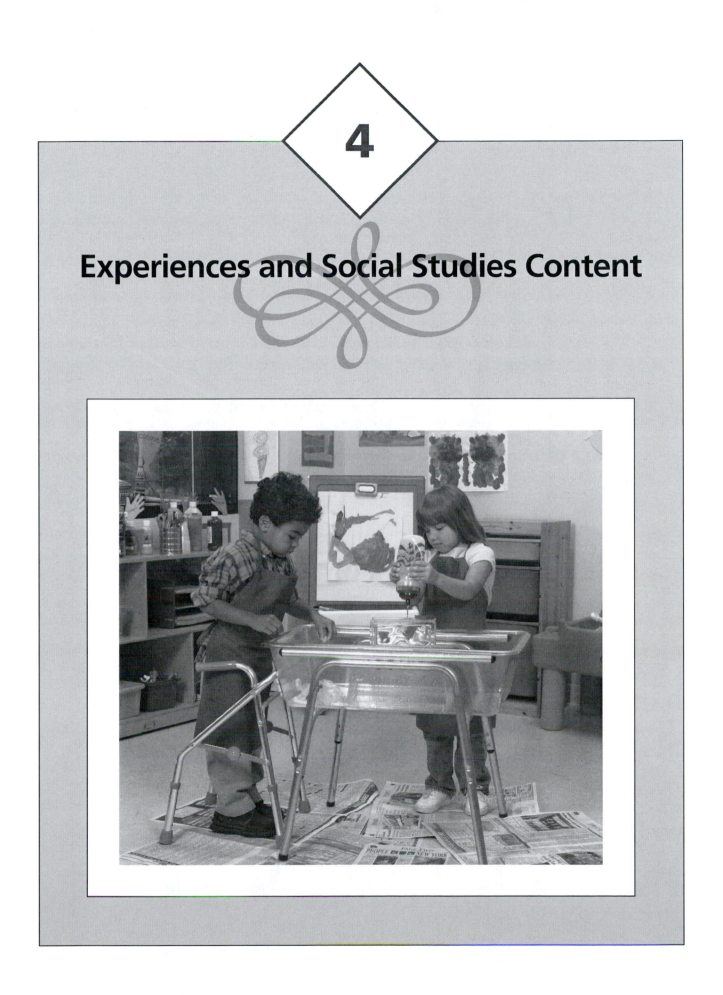

Experiences in order to be educative must lead out into an expanding world of subject-matter.

John Dewey, 1938, p. 37

Firsthand experiences in children's classrooms, homes, and communities form the foundation for their learning. These are like the first rungs on the learning ladder. However, unless a firsthand experience leads children to an ever-expanding world of new facts, information, and knowledge that was previously unfamiliar, children's learning will be limited. Thus, the next step on the learning ladder is the expansion and extension of the knowledge children have gained through their firsthand experiences into a fuller, richer, thicker, and more organized form (Dewey, 1938; Miettinen, 2000). This form gradually approximates the experts' understanding of a given subject matter or content area.

Teachers who enable children to turn their direct, firsthand experiences with their world into a coherent, organized body of knowledge are the double specialists of whom Piaget (1970) wrote. These are teachers who are engrossed in knowledge of each individual child, what each child knows, and how each learns. These teachers also have knowledge of the subject matter of the social studies. Then, because teachers are double specialists, they know how to bring children and subject matter content together.

KNOWLEDGE OF CHILDREN

Knowledge of some of the universals of children's growth, development, and learning is necessary (McAfee & Leong, 2001). There is wide variation, however, in children's growth, development, and learning. Some is due to the variation in the sociocultural context of children's lives; some to the variation in patterns of normal growth and development. Even though individual children develop differently, we know from research and theory that children in each age group share certain characteristics:

Three-Year-Olds

- have a vocabulary of about 2,000 to 4,000 words that expands daily.

- are learning to use listening skills as a means of learning about the world.

- can understand the concept of drawing and painting with uncontrolled scribbles that are one-directional and less repetitive than the scribbles of a 2-year-old.

- think in ways that are perceptually bound to one attribute and characteristic—an object can be blue, but not blue and small.

- are bound by egocentric thought—they are not "puffed up" with themselves; they simply do not understand that others have ideas and thoughts that may differ from theirs.

- play alongside others but not really with them.

Four-Year-Olds

- expand their vocabulary from 4,000 to 6,000 words and show more attention to abstract uses.

- use verbal commands to claim things; begin teasing.

- engage in conversation with others, considering the understanding of the other person.

- learn new vocabulary when it is related to their own experiences.

- know scribbles represent something and often name scribbles; can differentiate scribbles that look like writing from those meant to represent drawings.

- begin associative play, playing next to others but beginning to play together.

Five-Year-Olds

- are very articulate and can use language to control others, make plans, and solve problems.

- engage in lengthy conversations with others.

- are interested in letters and numbers, and are perhaps beginning to print or copy letters.

- count and know colors.

- recognize one can get meaning from the printed word.

- begin to play cooperatively, planning play and becoming able to sustain the play over time.

Teachers can use many resources to gain a better understanding of children's general growth and development. Authorities in the field of early childhood, such as Gesell, Ilg, and Ames, whose studies are reported in *Infant and Child in the Culture of Today* (1974), and Bredekamp and Copple, who wrote *Developmentally Appropriate Practice in Early Childhood Programs* (1997), have identified universal patterns of children's growth, development, and learning.

This universal information about children's growth and development informs teachers about the potentials and vulnerabilities of young children. This understanding tells us that, in general, the younger the child, the more wedded the child is to learning through firsthand interactions with the environment and others. Therefore, 3-, 4-, and 5-year-olds, still in the preoperational period of cognitive development, must rely on firsthand experiences in order to learn. As they grow and mature, however, they become increasingly more reliant on learning through symbols, through pictures, and through spoken and written language.

KNOWLEDGE OF THE SUBJECT MATTER— THE SOCIAL STUDIES

Knowledge of children alone is not enough if teachers are to expand and extend children's learning. If they are to take children further up the learning ladder, then they must also have a solid understanding of the subject matter they want children to learn.

Just as authorities in the field of early childhood have identified universals of children's growth, development, and learning, authorities in the field of social studies have likewise identified general facts, information, and knowledge key to social studies (National Council for the Social Studies [NCSS], 1994). Knowledge of these key concepts or themes that serve to organize the social studies guides teachers in the selection of firsthand experiences that will serve as a base for children's learning, as well as leads them in expanding and extending these firsthand experiences into more formal, conventional knowledge.

The social studies, defined as the integrated study of the social sciences and humanities to promote civic competence, is not a singular field. The very definition of the social studies indicates that social studies is an integrated field, one that involves a myriad of purposes and content.

> The social studies are the study of the political, economic, cultural, and environmental aspects of societies of the past, present, and future. For elementary school children as well as for all age groups social studies have several purposes. The social studies equip them with the knowledge and understanding of the past necessary for coping with the present and planning for the future, enable them to understand and participate effectively in their world, and explain their relationship to other people and to social, economic, and political institutions. Social studies can provide students with the skills for productive problem solving and decision making, as well as for assessing issues and making thoughtful value judgments. Above all, the social studies help students to integrate these skills and understanding into a framework for responsible citizen participation, whether in their play group, the school, the community, or the world. (NCSS, 1998, p. 2.)

As a result of this definition, the social studies can include content from

- anthropology, archaeology, economics
- geography, history, philosophy
- political science, psychology, religion
- sociology, humanities, mathematics
- the natural sciences

It seems overwhelming to ask young children to gain all of the knowledge, skills, and attitudes they will need to become citizens of a diverse, interdependent, democratic world. And yet it is critical to introduce children to the social studies during the period of early childhood. It is during the early years of life that children develop

- the dispositions to learn and continue to learn.
- the attitudes and values inherent in a democratic society.
- perceptions and preconcepts that form the foundation for the development of more conventional social studies concepts as children grow and mature.

It is not necessary or possible to include all of the content from the social studies in schools for young children. Teachers make choices. They organize children's experiences around the general themes identified by the National Council for the Social Studies, which makes the task seem less overwhelming. Ten themes of the National Council for the Social Studies have been identified; six of these themes serve to organize this book: (a) culture; (b) time, continuity, and change; (c) people, places, and environments; (d) individual development and identity; (e) individuals, groups, and institutions; (f) production, distribution, and consumption. See Chapter 1 for a description of each and how the chapters in this book correspond to the themes. The other social studies themes are:

Power, Authority, and Governance   Understanding the historical development of the structure of power, authority, and governance and their evolving functions in contemporary U.S. society and other nations of the world is essential for developing civic competence. In exploring this theme students confront questions such as: What is power? How is it gained, used, and justified? What is legitimate authority?

Global Connections   The realities of global interdependence require understanding of the increasingly important and diverse goal connections among world societies and frequent tension between national interests and global priorities. Students address such international issues as health care, the environment, human rights, economic competition and interdependence, age-old ethnic enmities, and political military alliances.

Science, Technology, and Society   Modern life as we know it would be impossible without technology and the science that supports it. But technology brings with it many questions: Is new technology better than old? How can we manage technology so that the greatest number of people can benefit? How can we preserve our fundamental values and beliefs in the midst of technological change?

Civic Ideals and Practices   An understanding of civic ideals and practices is essential to full participation in a democratic society. Each of the chapters in this book provides children with activities that provide a basis for setting classroom rules and expectations and determining how to balance the needs of individuals with those of the group.

BRINGING KNOWLEDGE OF CHILDREN AND CONTENT TOGETHER

To bring children and social studies concepts together, teachers first need to find out all they can about the social studies content they are planning to teach young children. To do so they might

Through interactions with people and books, children learn about different societies.

- read textbooks on the subject they want to teach young children.

- refer to the standards to help determine the underlying concepts that children can learn. Teachers could read books on the topic written for students in the primary grades. For example, one teacher noticed that children were interested in electricity, calling it magic. Because she herself was unsure of the concepts of electricity, and which could be made accessible to young children, she read books on electricity written for third graders to help her identify key concepts.

- ask authorities in the field to share their information and expertise.

- visit museums, watch videos or television, search the Web, or attend lectures or talks on the topic.

Teachers then need to find out what children already know and understand of the concepts key to the social studies themes. To do so, teachers can

- Interview children:

    For example, to study landforms on their earth, ask children to:

    Tell everything they know about the earth.

    Name landforms they see.

    Describe what the earth is like.

    Draw the things they see living and traveling on the earth.

    Explain how the earth was made.

    Tell why they think as they do.

- Ask children:

    What they already know about the earth they live on.

    What they would like to learn about the earth.

    How they think they could gain this knowledge.

    After study of the earth, ask children what they learned about their earth.

- Take a walk around the child's neighborhood:

    Develop an understanding of what the child has already experienced and how these experiences can be expanded into conventional knowledge.

    Talk to the child's family, asking about family experiences, what the child is interested in and likes doing, and what the child is not familiar with or needs to become familiar with.

    Observe children as they work and play, noting what themes are involved in their play and how they solve problems, use language, and interact with others and their world.

EXPANDING AND EXTENDING FIRSTHAND EXPERIENCES

Children's experiences with their world enable them to develop spontaneous, everyday concepts. This everyday, personal knowledge, however, does not automatically lead to a deeper understanding or more conventional ways of knowing. Rather, these concepts act like Velcro, hooking onto whatever new information, facts, and experiences children are given. The richer the new information, the greater the possibility for children to see the relationship of one fact to others and to form generalizations.

Vygotsky (1986) pointed out that at different developmental stages, children learn different things as they independently act on and interpret their environment, but other people also interact with children, affecting the course of their development and learning. He thought children operated at two levels of thought. One was the stage at which they could solve problems and think without the guidance of an adult or a more skilled peer. The second level was the stage at which the child could do the same task with adult help or guidance. He called this the potential developmental level. The distance between the two levels was termed the "zone of proximal development" (Vygotsky, 1986).

This means that by understanding children's existing ideas and social studies content, teachers can extend and expand children's knowledge by doing the following:

- Providing children with all kinds of books—poetry, literature, single-concept, picture, and reference books—that pertain to concepts children are studying. These may be openly displayed on a shelf or table, inviting children to extend and expand their ideas of a given concept. Children can use some of the books independently; others can be read to the entire group or to an individual child or two.

- Looking at pictures and other print media with children. Videos, photographs, movies, and slides, as well as pictures of places and things in, or not in, their environment can be examined and discussed to extend and expand children's knowledge.

- Showing children how they can do something. Teachers, working collaboratively with children, can demonstrate how to join two pieces of wood, use a tool, or play a game.

- Telling children a fact or piece of information that will enable them to make sense of their world. Social knowledge is different from abstract knowledge (Piaget & Inhelder, 1969). Social knowledge, such as "The name of this is chair" or "This is what we will do when we ride on the bus," is simply told to children. There is no way for them to construct it for themselves.

- Questioning children. Ask children what a thing is, why it is this way, and how it got this way to spur their thinking in a new or different way.

- Asking children to observe and listen to authorities show or tell about their field: A police officer can show children how the siren in her car works; a veterinarian can show how to care for a dog.

- Having children use the computer to learn a new skill or fact, find information, or communicate with others.

- Using language to extend and expand children's ideas. Supplying the names of things, describing them, and giving children words to describe their actions enable children to build new concepts.

- Adding another experience. Based on an understanding of children's ideas and concepts in a given discipline, add another real-life experience that will expand and extend these.

- Providing multiple opportunities for children to learn from one another. Children should be able to revisit their existing ideas of the subject matter by freely sharing their view of the world with others and arguing their point of view.

Children use the computer to find information and communicate with others.

Only through interactions with others can children critically consider their existing ideas and revise these to form more complex and conventional concepts of their world.

By respecting the children, how they learn, and the subject matter, teachers extend and expand children's existing knowledge. Teachers teach. Bredekamp and Rosegrant (1995) ask teachers "not to water down the learning experience even for the youngest child" (p. 22), but rather to build on children's existing knowledge and experience by assessing and supporting learning.

SUMMARY

Firsthand experiences enable children to construct everyday, spontaneous concepts. These concepts are like the first rung on a ladder of learning. The role of the teacher is to extend and expand these concepts into fuller, richer, more conventional knowledge. Teachers do this by developing an understanding of children and how they learn as well as a knowledge of content, and then bringing the two together.

Authorities in the social studies have identified themes or concepts key to the field. These are used by teachers to guide them as they extend and expand children's everyday concepts.

Concepts can be expanded and extended in a number of ways. Books, print media, the computer, and other technologies can be made available. Teachers can demonstrate skills or apply concepts and give children information that will enable them to reach a fuller understanding of themselves and the world in which they live.

PART TWO

Guides to Active Experiences

5

Different Kinds of Families

FOR THE TEACHER

◇ **What You'll Need to Know**

Very few teachers are meeting and greeting what has been called the traditional nuclear family—mother, father, and two children. When Ms. Knight came home from the first Family Night at her childcare center, she commented to her mother that she had never seen so many different kinds of families. "Each child came through the door with a different kind of family. I had no idea what to expect next." Fortunately, Ms. Knight accepted the diversity of families represented in her classroom as an exciting opportunity. Yet, she believed that it would be challenging to find resources and children's books that represented the home experiences and cultures of all of her students. Even at that, she had to be sensitive about discussing homes since there was a homeless child in the class and one who was living temporarily in foster care.

Today's teacher may expect to work with children from the following kinds of complex family structures:

- **Single parent.**   Single parents account for about 27% of households with children under age 18. Children of single parents may differ widely in their home situation. Some single parents are divorced, some are guardians or a grandparent, others have adopted children either from the United States or internationally (which may result in a mixed-race family), and others are lesbian and gay parents. They may be single-parent fathers or single-parent mothers. Clearly, it is not enough to plan activities for children with just the term *single parent* in mind.

- **Both parents.**   These families may be of the traditional nuclear family type, but frequently children come from multiracial and multiethnic families. According to the Center for Health Statistics, the number of multiracial babies born since the 1970s has increased more than 260%, compared to a 15% increase of single-race babies (Wardle, 2003). Mixed-race families are an ever-growing part of our national landscape and represent a variety of races. As mentioned, international adoptions are also creating mixed-race families. According to Wardle (2003), parents of young multiethnic and multiracial children often see early childhood programs as insensitive to their family's unique needs. They also believe that teachers have a lack of information about them.

- **Gay- and lesbian-headed/unmarried partner families.**   About one-third of lesbian households and one-fifth of gay male households have children. Clay (2004) found that these parents wanted emotional security and an experienced staff for their children. But they also wanted them to be part of the general community, not outsiders. Many of the lesbian and gay parents thought that adoption issues were more important to their children than issues about having a parent who is lesbian or gay.

- **Extended families.**   Extended families are created when a nuclear family or single-parent family lives with any extended family members. Often children of this kind of family need activities that focus on intergenerational contacts and issues. These families may also be multiracial or multiethnic.

A subtype of the previously listed family types may be what is termed a *blended family,* which is usually created when formerly divorced parents marry new partners. The notion that families "blend" without some stress has been disproved. Children from blended families need a good deal of support.

All of these families are part of a culture. Culture has been defined as an integrated pattern of human behavior that includes thoughts, communication, languages, practices, beliefs, values, customs, courtesies, rituals, roles, relationships, and expected behaviors of a racial, ethnic, religious, or social group. Also included in the definition is the ability to translate this culture to succeeding generations (Georgetown University Child Development Center, 1989). Many different kinds of families expect that important parts of their culture be preserved for their children. This is another important function of the school in conjunction with families. Yet, it is also important to recognize that families change.

◇ **Key Concepts, Goals, and Objectives Based on CTB and Curriculum Standards for the Social Studies**

These are based on individual development and identity, self-knowledge, social skills, and the motivation to learn. More specifically,

- Children will develop an understanding of the basic functions of a family.

- Children reared in different family types will develop healthy self-concepts.

- Children will value different kinds of families.

- Children will form positive relationships with children from different kinds of families.

- Children will describe the unique features of their nuclear family.

- Children will describe the unique features of their extended family.

- Children will describe the unique features of their single-parent family.

- Children will describe the unique features of their blended family.

◇ **What You'll Need**

As in Chapter 12, Valuing Diversity, activities for children that develop awareness and understanding of different kinds of families help the teacher to develop an antibias classroom. The teacher will want to be aware of ethical responsibilities to families. A good book that reinforces what good teachers know about cultural sensitivity, building relationships of mutual trust between the school and home, and establishing open lines for respectful communication with families is Feeney and Freeman's *Ethics and the Early Childhood Educator: Using the NAEYC Code* (1999). A must resource with an up-to-date and realistic approach to helping the teacher grow as a culturally responsive educator is Copple's *A World of Difference: Readings on Teaching Young Children in a Diverse Society* (2003).

Children's Books

There are many children's books that deal directly or indirectly with children and divorce, adoption, international adoption, multiracial and multiethnic parents, interracial identity, lesbian and gay parents or caregivers, blended families, single-parent fathers, single-parent mothers, and various types of extended families. Some are better than others. For example, many people like Laura Kransy and Marc Brown's *Dinosaur's Divorce* and Kathy Parkinson's *Mamma and Daddy Bear's Divorce*. Ms. Green read these books to her class of 4-year-olds. Then she overheard several children discussing what these animal divorces had to do with them. They expressed: "Animals live different from us! They don't need a divorce." "My Daddy is not a dinosaur." "The dinosaurs are silly."

Another widely used, but controversial, book is P. Mandelbaum's *You Be Me, I'll Be You.* Here the black child and white father use makeup to change skin color because the child doesn't like being black. Is this the message that teachers want to send? Teachers will need to formulate some standards for the books that they use in the classroom with children. See Chapter 12 for some ideas. At the most basic level, books should treat all family types with respect and sensitivity.

Some of the best children's books are:

Adoff, A. (1992). *Black is brown is tan.* New York: Harper/Collins Juvenile Books.

Cox, J. (2003). *My family plays music.* New York: Holiday House.

Davol, M. (1993). *Black, white, just right!* Morton Grove, IL: Albert Whitman & Co.

Friedman, I. R. (1984). *How my parents learned to eat.* Boston, MA: Houghton Mifflin Co.

Hamanaka, S. (1994). *All the colors of the earth.* New York: Morrow Junior Books.

Igus, T. (1996). *Two Mrs. Gibsons.* San Francisco, CA: Children's Book Press.

Johnson, A. (2004). *The first part last.* New York: Simon and Schuster Books for Young People.

Lewis, R. (2002). *I love you like crazy cakes.* Boston: Little Brown.

Mandelbaum, P. (1993). *You be me, I'll be you.* La Jolla, CA: Kane/Miller Books.

Newman, L. (2000). *Heather has two mommies.* Los Angeles, CA: Alyson Publications.

Pellegrini, N. (1991). *Families are different.* New York: Holiday House.

Skutch, R. (1995). *Who's in a family?* Berkeley, CA: Tricycle Press.

Smith, C. L. (2000). *Jingle dancer.* New York: Morrow Junior Books.

Steptoe, J., Illus. (1998). *In Daddy's arms I am tall: African Americans celebrating fathers.* New York: Lee and Low Books.

A child and her father can do the ironing.

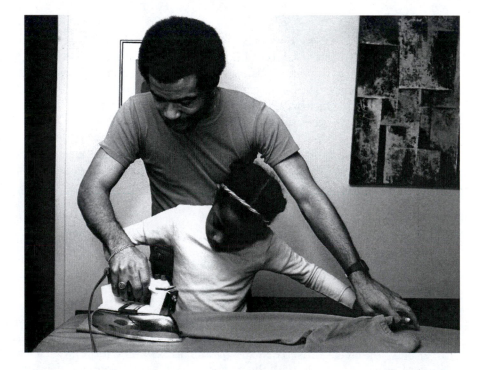

Wilhoite, M. (1990). *Daddy's roommate.* Los Angeles, CA: Alyson Publications.

Woodson, J. (2005). *Coming on home soon.* New York: GP Putnam's Son's/Penguin Young Readers Group.

Other Things You'll Need

- You will need to examine your attitudes toward families of various types. If you do have negative attitudes about some kinds of families it is probably because you see your responsibility to the children first and believe somehow that they could be harmed by a particular family style. Reflect on the functions of a family and determine if each family type is performing those functions but in a somewhat different way. For example, in Toyomi Igus's *Two Mrs. Gibsons,* the young girl's father is African American and her mother is Japanese. The book compares her grandmother (father's mother) and her mother. The child says "I once knew two Mrs. Gibsons. They were very different but they had a lot in common. They both loved my Daddy and they both loved me."

  Similarly, Robert Skutch's *Who's in a Family?* discusses many different family structures. The conclusion is that families can look different from one another. Even in the same family, family members can look different from one another, but they all can participate in important family activities that support family members.

- You'll need to review and possibly revise your attitudes about teacher/family communications. Also take a good look at the materials that you send to parents. Do your newsletters reflect the diversity in the class and at home and are they translated into the languages reflected in the classroom? What about letters home? Your bulletin boards? Are diverse families adequately informed of and welcomed to conferences and school programs? Do conferences represent a genuine effort to bridge home and school? Are your school programs of interest to various kinds of families? Are they designed to encourage families to communicate with you and each other? Have you created time for small family discussion groups and staff/family discussions? Topics should not be teacher generated. Be sure to consult with families about topics of importance to them.

- Examine the environment of the classroom. Are materials bias-free? Are a variety of family styles depicted on the walls and in the library corner? Are the languages of the children represented in displays and books?

The Home-School Connection

In working with different kinds of families and getting them to embrace the teacher's goals for a diverse classroom, nothing is more important than the home-school connection. Teachers must learn to be empathetic and patient in forging relationships with families. They will want to communicate that families are respected, as are their decisions, ideas, and values. They make time for their concerns, encourage their questions, and address each one with the consideration it deserves (Kaufman, 2003).

Strum (2003) points to the difficulties in establishing intercultural communication in child care. "I knew that culture means more than holidays and food; it includes all the subtle patterns of communication—verbal and nonverbal—that people use every day. I noticed how easily I valued cultural diversity in the abstract or in the form of occasional holidays, yet how readily I rejected cultural differences when they appeared in the form of parents' different approaches to child rearing." Through a parent/teacher dialogue project, families and teachers feel more trust and connection with each other. Teachers will also want to listen carefully to the issues of gay and lesbian parents, adoptive parents, and families of different racial and ethnic composition.

◇ **Evaluating and Assessing Children's Learning**

Assessing children's progress in understanding and valuing different kinds of families will be an ongoing process. The teachers will want to observe and interview individuals and groups using structured instruments. Portfolios should be used to chart the child's learning over time. Observation of children's play—particularly in the housekeeping area—should give the teacher some good insights into how children are assimilating and dealing with the curriculum based on the teacher's objectives concerning knowledge of families and positive feelings toward different kinds of families. The more structured evaluation on the tear out sheet on page 66 may be used at different points in the school year. Even more important in assessing the curriculum may be the extent to which it is being positively reinforced by the children's families. Why not send parents a short questionnaire asking how they like some of your activities?

──────────────── **FOR THE CHILDREN** ────────────────

◇ **Standard 1. Understanding What Families Do**

◆ Encourage children to draw pictures of what their families do and what they do for them. Challenge them to think of things other than "fun" activities. Ask some questions: Where do you get your food? Your clothes? Who hugs you when you are sad? Be careful to support children with difficult family situations. Create a T-chart with things that families do for children in one column and who does them in the other. For example, with "Who hugs you when you are sad?" it could be "father, mother, grandmother," and so forth. In other words, a wide variety of people can meet a child's needs.

Things families do for children	Who does thesethings
Shop for their food	mother, father, grandmother, grandfather, aunt

Another family function is to provide shelter or a home. Here the teacher must be careful. Wellhousen (2003) suggests that the following concepts introduced to children about homes are incorrect and outdated:

1. All children have homes.

2. A home is a house in a neighborhood.

3. The immediate members of the child's family all live together.

4. Children have only one place they call home.

5. Home is a safe, loving, good place to be.

Keeping these concepts in mind, after the teacher is thoroughly familiar with her children's homes and their concepts of home, she may develop a KWL chart. It might look like this: What do we **k**now about the places children live? What **w**ould we like to know? What have we **l**earned? Some teachers like to add: What do we still want to learn?

Know	Would like to know	Learned
Children live in houses Most children have homes	Do they live in apartments? Can they have more than one?	They do live in apartments They can–with mother part time and father part time

After developing the chart, plan a walk around the immediate neighborhood, noting that not all of the children or their teachers live here. Children and teachers can discuss and take notes on types of homes—apartment buildings, single houses, row or town houses, and so forth. If possible, the children (with the help of their parents) can take pictures of their homes for display in the classroom. The teacher will want to emphasize that there is no universally right place to live.

An important family function involves working to provide for the needs of the family. Have the children

◆ Create a bar graph depicting the various types of work done by their family members. They should include mothers, fathers, and any extended family members that contribute to the family.

◆ Ask children to think of some people who live in their community such as police officers, firefighters, or grocery store workers. Explain that they are all members of families. Ask children what these people look like. Have them draw pictures of these people emphasizing the differences. Make sure that you have crayons or markers to represent various skin colors.

◆ Using old magazines and catalogs, have the children create collages depicting various workers. Have children select people of different genders and racial backgrounds. Have each child list which groups are represented in his/her collage. Attach the lists to the bottom of the collage when they are displayed. Compare the lists.

◇ **Standard 2. Learning and Describing the Unique Features of Different Families**

It is not possible for the teacher to acquaint young children with each possible family type. Nor does the teacher want to single out particular children as being adopted or the child of a single parent. Some children will speak freely about their family situation after reading a book about families or doing a family-related activity. The following activities should form a basis for describing different kinds of families and learning to value diversity.

◆ Read Rose Lewis' *I Love You Like Crazy Cakes.* In this story the Caucasian adoptive mother tells her story about how she adopted her daughter from China. Ask the children why they think the mother went through so much to adopt this baby. Children may answer that she needed a baby to love. Ask them what the baby needed (in this case, a mother). Rose Lewis introduces the baby to family and friends. Have the children dictate a sentence or two on how they would introduce the new baby from China. What would they want to tell their family and friends about the baby? Some children may want to share their introductions.

◆ Much like the previous book, Jamie Lee Curtis' *Tell Me Again About the Night I Was Born* is a positive portrayal of adoption, this time with a mother and a father. Read the book to the whole class or in small groups. Have the children ask their families about the night they were born or write a letter to parents asking them to tell their children. Create a bulletin board entitled "The Night I Was Born." If possible, include a picture of each child in the center of the short story. If some children cannot obtain the information, have them create a story about the night that they were born.

◆ Read one of the 12 poems from *In Daddy's Arms I Am Tall: African Americans Celebrating Fathers.* Have each child write or dictate a sentence explaining what is special about a father or a grandfather. Record these on chart paper. Then have each child write or dictate a sentence about some things fathers and grandfathers can teach children.

◆ Suggest that there are ways to honor or celebrate a parent (father or mother) or grandparent different from the commercial Mother's or Father's Day. Have the children in small groups think of ways to celebrate their parents or grandparents. List these on chart paper. Suggest that the children's ideas will be used in a planned Celebration of Families at the end of the year.

◆ Every few days have children add something to the celebration list such as a recipe they will make from a multicultural cookbook, or a button for their family members to wear. Children should pick the message for the button. Children may also make artwork using all media including clay and wood constructions and dedicate them to their family members.

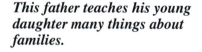

This father teaches his young daughter many things about families.

◆ Children are interested in the lives of the authors of children's books. Read A. Adoff's *Black Is Brown Is Tan.* Ask the children why Adoff would want to write a book like this. Suggest that the class in small groups find out more about his life. Assist the children is researching his life. Point out that he was Caucasian, and that his wife, Virginia Hamilton, was African American. His children were a combination of their traits as exhibited in their skin color. Leave his books in the library corner so that the children have an opportunity to examine them at their leisure. After reading his books, ask the class if they think Adoff was happy about his children's skin color. Go over the titles again. Were his children happy? Examine the drawings. Draw conclusions.

◆ Another author whom children might explore is Marguerite Davol, who wrote *Black, White, Just Right.* Have the class guess why she wrote this book. In this case, Davol's Caucasian son married a black Kenyan woman. Ask the children what she wanted to tell the reader about her grandchildren. They should answer that they were "just right." There is a picture of Davol with her grandchildren on the inner cover. Discuss whether any of the children in the class have families that look like that and are "just right." The book is written so that the children can chant "just right" throughout.

◆ Read Friedman's *How My Parents Learned to Eat.* For the young girl, eating some days with chopsticks and some days with knives and forks is natural. Ask if any of the children eat with different implements or eat foods of different cultures. Children may not be aware of what foods represent different cultures, so the teacher may want to be ready with pictures, descriptions, or even the actual foods to taste. Older children could visit restaurants in the community. Record the responses. For the bulletin board, make a chart of different foods the children eat and how they eat them. Have the children illustrate the different kinds of foods. For the young narrator of this children's book, to eat in this way is the best of all possible worlds.

◆ Continue to introduce the children in your class to various kinds of foods that are representative of different cultures. Many are easy for the children to make such as hummus, quesadillas, and guacamole. The children may use pita bread or tortilla chips as implements. See L. J. Colker's *The Cooking Book: Fostering Young Children's Learning and Delight* (2005) for easy recipes for a variety of foods from different cultures. The foods may be served at the Celebration of Families.

◇ **Standard 3. Children Will Form Positive Relationships with Children from Different Kinds of Families**

◆ Describe the class as an extended family where each student is a valued member. Ask students why the class could be considered a family. Make a banner for the Celebration of Families entitled "We Are a Family." Put it on the bulletin board or hang it from the ceiling or a doorway. Have strings extending from the banner representing each child. Have each child create something that represents him/her. It could be a drawing, a photograph, or a symbol of some sort. Assist children in designing something that represents their personal worth and identity.

◆ Hold a Celebration of Families. Begin by sending a letter home to families informing them of your plans and asking them to come together to discuss their ideas for the event. If a family cannot come to the planning session, invite them to send their ideas to you. Emphasize in your letter (p. 65) that each family's input is important to the success of the event and how important it is to celebrate family diversity.

Celebration of Families

◆ Have a parallel planning session with the children. Explain how all of the activities that they have been doing can be a part of the celebration. Chart the ideas. Encourage each child to speak up for his/her idea. Try to make each child feel important and incorporate all suggestions, if possible.

◆ The Celebration of Families will need an exhibition of children's art representing different family cultures. Children love to make art, but they should be exposed to good art through children's books to give them ideas and techniques. Introduce the children to the following books.

Garza, C. L. (1993). *Family pictures/Cuadros de familia.* Children's Book Press.
O'Connor, J. (2003). *Mary Cassatt: Family pictures.* Grosset & Dunlap.
Schaefer, A. R. (2003). *Diego Rivera.* Heinemann.

Discuss how the art is the same/different. How are the families the same/different? For example, Claire, who studies Mary Cassatt, compares her pictures to her own family. C. L. Carza's pictures are of a quite different poor, rural Hispanic family. Yet, both books express a love of families and the things they do. Make a Venn diagram (Figure 5.1).

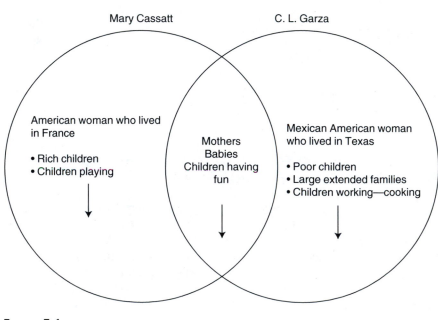

FIGURE 5.1
Venn Diagram

Have the children create their own family pictures for the celebration using the ideas from the children's books and artwork that the teacher has displayed. This may include prints, sculpture, textiles by artists of various backgrounds that reflect the aesthetic environment and the culture of the families represented in the classroom, and pictures of groups in the community and in the country as a whole (Neugebauer, 1987).

For added interest and beauty, assist the children in framing their pictures. Frames can be created or constructed from a variety of materials including colored construction paper; discarded paper of varying textures, colors, and materials; pages from a discarded wallpaper book; paper plates; Styrofoam trays; box lids; burlap; and other materials. Consult C. Seefeldt's *Creating Rooms of Wonder* (2002) for framing ideas and techniques. Make sure the pictures are labeled and displayed. Seefeldt (2002) suggests that asymmetrical displays are more inviting than artwork displayed in uniform rows.

◆ The celebration will also need music and movement. Both are reflective of many aspects of culture as previously defined. First, provide the children with a variety of instruments from different cultures and countries. If possible, families may lend instruments and demonstrate their use. The music departments of local colleges and universities may have resources to assist you. The teacher may want to make sure that rules are established for the safe and respectful use of different instruments. Children should only handle them in small groups of two or three. Help children to compare and contrast the instruments and their sounds.

◆ Make your own instruments. Using paper plates, plastic cups, or pie tins, have the children place such materials as rice, sand, pennies, marbles, or beans between them, then staple them together. These maracas can be used to accompany familiar chants or songs.

◆ Read C. L. Smith's *Jingle Dancer.* Jenna, a Native American who is comfortable with the dominant culture as well, decides that she would like to honor a family tradition by jingle dancing. She collects jingles from family and friends but not too many so that others won't have a chance. The jingles are cone shaped. Make some jingles and attach them to the children's clothes. Try jingle dancing.

◇ **Reflecting**

Children reflect on a theme by organizing all of their experiences with that theme and communicating to others what they have learned. A festive family party at the school is an ideal way for children to do this. They can organize their experiences in various ways:

◆ Have the children decide which artwork relating to families to exhibit. They will need to decide how they will arrange their work and where they will put it for family viewing. In the process, children will discuss the different family types that are depicted.

◆ Children will decide what types of music they will play on the CD player. They may organize a short musical play where they feature their homemade instruments and songs, chants, and dances learned from different cultures. Children can invite families to join in the musical fun. Teaching different kinds of music to their families reinforces children's learning.

◆ Have the children decide what refreshments they would like to serve at the party. Remind them of the different foods that they have sampled throughout the year. A chart can be made with pictures of various foods labeled as to culture. Foods such as hummus can be made at school and children can take a field trip to purchase more complex items such as Chinese dumplings.

A culminating event such as a family party helps children to reflect upon and apply their knowledge of different kinds of families.

◇ Extending and Expanding to the Primary Grades

Primary-age children can understand that they can belong to more than one group. This makes many types of activities possible. The purpose is to help students to recognize (a) that they can be unique while belonging to many groups and (b) most of us belong to diverse groups. The following are examples:

◆   Have students identify the groups to which they belong and help them in charting them on a pie graph. The graph should assist them in understanding that each of these groups is a piece of them. To begin this activity, the teacher will need to provide students with a variety of examples. Students should then name the groups that they belong to and record them on a chart. Assist them in identifying groups such as African American, Italian American, or child in a family. To make this an active experience, have the children get up each time a different group that applies to them is called. Make sure there are at least one or more groups for everyone. After calling the groups, ask children what they observed.

◆   Next, have children decide how important each of the groups is to them. Color the groups bigger or smaller using different colors of crayons. Then label the groups. Exhibit the pie charts on the bulletin board to illustrate the diversity of the class (Figure 5.2).

◆   Primary-age children can discuss feelings and empathize with others. Read Jacqueline Woodson's *Coming Home Soon*. During World War II, women are needed to fill

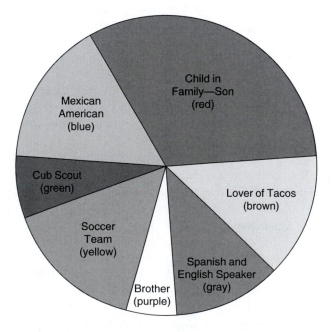

FIGURE 5.2
Pie Chart: I Belong to Many Groups

men's jobs. Ada Ruth and her grandma keep up their daily routine and wait for Mama to come home. Ask the children why Grandma can fill the place of Mama. In what ways can she not take Mama's place? Ask them to dictate a sentence about how they would feel if they were Ada Ruth.

◆ Read A. Johnson's *The First Part Last*. Bobby, a 16-year-old artist, finds himself a single parent raising a daughter. Ask students to think about Bobby's dilemma. What should he do? Why? Where does personal responsibility become important? Can Bobby raise a daughter? At what cost? Is the cost worth it?

◆ The teacher may pose other questions based on hypothetical family situations. Jim's mother recently married a man with two children, a boy and a girl. How might Jim feel? What things would help Jim and the other children to get along and feel wanted by their parents? When they divorced, Brenda's parents agreed that she would come to one parent's home for half of each week. What problems could that make for Brenda? (For example, if she left her backpack at her father's house). What could her parents do to help her with her situation? Anita's elderly aunt recently came to live with the family. She misses her home and her old friends. What could Anita do to help her? What could the aunt do for Anita? Evan's parents just adopted a baby girl from Russia. How do you think that Evan might feel? Does it matter that the baby  is from Russia? Anna's mother is Japanese and her father is Caucasian. Children keep asking her questions about how that could happen. How could you help Anna to answer those questions? Use the various kinds of charts and graphs mentioned in the book to record the answers. You might want to work on problems such as this over the course of the year. If so, create a bulletin board or "Family Center" where children can go to revise answers that they gave before and add more or better solutions.

◆ Read Judy Cox's *My Family Plays Music*. This extended multiracial family represents a rainbow of skin tones. But what about their musical tastes? Prior to reading the book, have the children guess which family members prefer which instruments. Then have them pair the instruments with the family member. Discuss how members of such a large extended family could have such different tastes in music. How does this illustrate how we can be alike and still different? Ask the children to come up with sentences describing the advantages of diversity. For example, wouldn't it be boring to only listen to a marching band? Bluegrass music?

◆ Plan a Celebration of Families for primary-age children. These children are old enough to discuss their plans and vote on their choices for music, food, and so forth. Their families should also be included in the plans. The teacher may have to intervene to make sure that each family type is represented at the Celebration.

◇ **Documenting Children's Learning**

Children's learning is documented in their charts, lists, stories, exhibits, and performances. A web that hangs constantly in the classroom reminds children of changes in their skills, attitudes, and behavior as a result of their unit, Different Kinds of Families. Children should be encouraged to add to the web as the year progresses and they are exposed to different experiences.

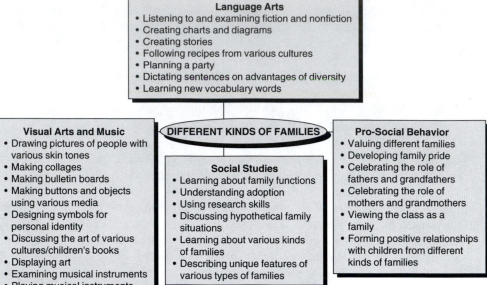

Language Arts
- Listening to and examining fiction and nonfiction
- Creating charts and diagrams
- Creating stories
- Following recipes from various cultures
- Planning a party
- Dictating sentences on advantages of diversity
- Learning new vocabulary words

DIFFERENT KINDS OF FAMILIES

Visual Arts and Music
- Drawing pictures of people with various skin tones
- Making collages
- Making bulletin boards
- Making buttons and objects using various media
- Designing symbols for personal identity
- Discussing the art of various cultures/children's books
- Displaying art
- Examining musical instruments
- Playing musical instruments
- Dancing
- Making musical instruments

Social Studies
- Learning about family functions
- Understanding adoption
- Using research skills
- Discussing hypothetical family situations
- Learning about various kinds of families
- Describing unique features of various types of families

Pro-Social Behavior
- Valuing different families
- Developing family pride
- Celebrating the role of fathers and grandfathers
- Celebrating the role of mothers and grandmothers
- Viewing the class as a family
- Forming positive relationships with children from different kinds of families

Parent Letter

Date _____

Dear Families:

Your children and their teachers have decided to have a Celebration of Families. As you know, the idea builds on what we have been studying all year—Different kinds of families. We appreciate your efforts to provide us with materials for our work and assist your children in finding out more about their families.

We have decided on _____ at _____ in the _____ at school. Your whole family is invited, and transportation will be provided for anyone who needs it. The children have decided that they want food and drink of different cultures (some of which they will prepare), art, music and dance, and some special decorations, displays, and gifts to honor you.

We would very much like to have you work with us. Please let us know if you are available either next week or the following (day or evening) to offer your suggestions and help us with the planning. This is for you and you should be a part of it. We can schedule more than one discussion, if needed. So, if you would send back the attached card, we will arrange the times.

The children are very excited and so are we. Looking forward to seeing you.

Sincerely,

_____

I would be available to work with you _____ next week
_____ the following week on (days):

I can come _____ Morning _____ Afternoon _____ Evening.

Signed _____

Date: _____

Name: _____

Age of Child: _____

Individual Evaluation of Children's Knowlege of and Feelings About Different Kinds of Families

	Always	Sometimes	Never
When asked, articulates the basic functions of a family	_____	_____	_____
Exhibits an understanding of the basic family function through art, music, storywriting	_____	_____	_____
Shows an awareness of different kinds of families in discussions and classroom activities	_____	_____	_____
When appropriate, shows pride in his/her family type	_____	_____	_____
Is anxious to participate in activities about different types of families	_____	_____	_____
Plays frequently with children of different kinds of families	_____	_____	_____
Is anxious to participate in a Celebration of Families	_____	_____	_____
Uses vocabulary consistent with new concepts about families	_____	_____	_____
Expresses opinions appropriately	_____	_____	_____
Expresses feelings about family situations	_____	_____	
Shows a preference for a particular kind of family. If so, which	_____		

Which of the following is most effective in helping this child to understand and value different kinds of families? Please check.

Children's books

Art projects

Informal discussions

Formal discussions

Music and dance

Teacher-directed lessons

Field experiences

Other

6

The Past Is Present
History for Young Children

─────────────────────── **FOR THE TEACHER** ───────────────────────

◇ **What You'll Need to Know**

"I don't get afraid when I have a nightmare because I know morning comes next," 3-year-old Sabrina explained. Young children like Sabrina have a limited sense of time. They can tell you what will happen before or after a given routine, "I know morning will come," but they confuse the meaning of the terms *today, tomorrow,* and *yesterday.* "Once upon a time," and "A long time ago," are phrases that seem to sum up young children's concepts of the passage of time.

For young children, then, the study of history is based not on an abstract and conventional sense of time, but the study of their own lives. By beginning with children's own past, the study of history connects each child with his or her roots and develops a sense of personal belonging in the greet sweep of human experiences (NCHS, 1994).

Children are very interested in the past; that is, when it is their own past. Who hasn't heard a child beg for just one more story about when he or she was little long, long ago? This interest alone would be reason to include the study of history in the early childhood curriculum. History is necessary for other reasons, however. A sense of the past, the ability to think historically, is critical if children are to develop self-identity, to see their own place in the stream of time and one's connectedness with all of humankind.

Children can begin to develop preconcepts of present time, past time, and the long, long ago. Children can also study the effects of the passage of time, observing and exploring the effects of change on their own lives. Perhaps most critical is the fact that children can learn to use the methods of the historian. Even the youngest can begin to identify problems, collect information, observe, and reach conclusions about not only their own pasts, but the pasts of others.

◇ **History Standards: Key Concepts**

- Time and its passage can be measured.

- There is a difference between past, present, and future time.

- As time passes, changes occur.

- Children use the methods of the historian to identify problems, collect information, observe, and reach conclusions about the past.

◇ **Goals and Objectives**

Children will begin the measure of time using arbitrary and conventional measures.

Children will be able to distinguish the difference between present, past, and future time.

Children will learn to observe and record change, developing the idea that change is continuous and always present by talking about the changes in their lives.

Children will ask questions, collect information, observe, and reach conclusions about the past.

◇ **What You'll Need**

Visit the National Center for History in the School's website (*www.sscnet.ucla.edu/nchs/*) and obtain a copy of *National Standards for History for Grades K–4: Expanding Children's World in Time and Space.* This resource is an excellent guide to planning appropriate activities that introduce children to concepts of history. This information can also be retrieved by contacting:

The National Center for History in the Schools
Department of History
University of California, Los Angeles
405 Hilgard Ave.
Los Angeles, CA 90095-1473
FAX: 310 267-2103

The American Association for State and Local History's website (*www.aaslh.org/*) provides resources and leadership support for preserving and interpreting state and local history. To find out more about local and state museums and other history resources, you can contact the American Association for State and Local History:

AASLH
1717 Church St
Nashville, TN 37203-2991
FAX: 615-327-9013
www.aaslh.org

Supplies

To involve children in measuring time, you will need stopwatches, an hourglass, a kitchen timer, and old alarm clocks. These do not really have to work, or be exact, because the point is simply for children to learn that time is measured. Keep clipboards and markers handy for children to sketch, record their experiences, or just pretend to write.

You will also need paper and drawing supplies so children can make books and murals and draw in order to reflect on their experiences.

A digital camera or other way of taking photos of children at work and play is valuable. The photos enable children to recall past experiences and talk and reflect about them. Photos are also useful in documenting and evaluating children's work.

Children's Books

The National Center for History in the Schools believes that children's literature serves an important place in teaching young children history. History becomes especially accessible and interesting to children when approached through stories, myths, legends, and biographies that capture children's imaginations and immerse them in times and cultures of the recent and long-ago past.

Contact the Children's Book Council and the National Council for the Social Studies for lists of history books: Children's Book Council, *www.cbcbooks.org.*

The following books are used in this chapter:

Brill, M. T. (1993). *Allen Jay and the underground railroad.* New York: First Avenue Editions.

Burton, V. (1978). *Little house.* New York: Houghton Mifflin Company.

DePaola, T. (1996). *Legend of the Bluebonnets: An old tale of Texas.* New York: Putnam Juvinelle.

DePaola, T. (1998). *Nana upstairs, Nana downstairs.* New York: Putnam.

Foran, J. (2003). *Native-American life.* New York: Weigl Publishers, Inc.

George, J. C. (1999). *Morning, noon, and night.* New York: Harper & Row.

Glazer, T. (1973). *Eye winker, Tom tinker, chin chopper: Fifty musical fingerplays.* Garden City, NY: Doubleday.

Hearne, B., & Andersen, B. (1997). *Seven brave women.* New York: Greenwillow.

Hutchins, P. (1983). *You'll soon grow into them.* New York: Greenwillow.

Johnson, A. (1992). *Tell me a story, mama.* New York: Orchard Books.

Johnson, A. (1996). *The leaving morning.* New York: Orchard Books.

Kelso, R. (1993). *Days of courage: The Little Rock story.* New York: Raintree.

Milne, A. A. (1927). *Now we are six.* London: Dutton & Co.

Osborne, M. P. (1999). *Buffalo before breakfast.* New York: Random House Children's Books.

Parnall, P. (1987). *The apple tree.* New York: Macmillan.

Shiller, P. B., Silberg, J., & Wright, D. C. (2001). *The complete book of rhymes, songs, poems, finger plays and chants: Over 700 selections.* Beltsville, MD: Gryphon House.

Steptoe, J. (2000). *In daddy's arms I am tall: African Americans celebrating fathers.* New York: Lee & Low Books, Inc.

Taberski, S., & Doniger, N. (1996). *Morning, noon, and night: Poems to fill your day.* New York: Mondo Publishing.

Taylor, M. D. (2003). *Song of the trees.* New York: Puffin.

Van Leeuwen, J. (1995). *Across the wide dark sea: The Mayflower journey.* New York: Dial Books.

Walker, S. M. (1998). *The 18 penny goose.* New York: HarperCollins Juvenile Books.

Wells, R., & McPhail, D. M. (2001). *Night sounds, morning colors.* New York: Dial Books for Young Readers.

Wells, R., & Wells, T. (2003). *The house in the mail.* New York: Puffin Books.

Wyeth, S. D. (2002). *Something beautiful.* New York: Doubleday Dell.

The Home-School Connection

The involvement of families is necessary in the study of history. Each family has something unique from the past to give to its children. Ask families to let you use the rich uniqueness of their individual histories as a springboard for learning history in the classroom. For this purpose, you could use or modify the letter to parents on the tear out sheet at the end of this chapter (p. 80).

◇   Evaluating and Assessing Children's Learning

Observe the children and listen as they talk and play together. Carry self-stick notes with you or keep them around the room. Use these to record when children use time words and the extent to which their usage is accurate.

Record any instances of children pretending to measure or actually measuring time as they play indoors or outdoors. Record any instances of children asking questions, identifying problems, collecting data, and reaching conclusions about the past.

You can transcribe your notes to a form, or put them in children's portfolios to document their growing concepts of time. The tear out sheets titled "Time Words," "Measuring Time," "Methods of the Historian," and "History Concepts" at the end of this chapter (pp. 81–84) can be used to record your observations.

FOR THE CHILDREN

◇ Standard 1. Measuring the Passage of Time

Generally, 3- and 4-year-old children measure the passage of time through the routines of the day, week, month, and year. The goal is to introduce children to the idea that time passes and can be measured.

◆ Start with some simple activities and conversations.

- Establish routines that are constant and at the same time flexible. Talk about the routines: "After we play outside we'll have a snack." "Now it's time to put our things away and get ready for lunch."

- Talk about and make plans for a weekend when children are not at school. Ask them what they will do on the weekend. Name the days.

- Mark special days on a calendar. For example, 3- and 4-year-olds are not ready to keep track of the days, or interested in doing so, but they can be involved in placing a picture of a cake and candle labeled with their name or a friend's name on the calendar to show when it's their birthday or their friend's birthday.

- Make a chain of paper rings with one ring for each day before a special event. You might make a chain representing the days before a trip, a holiday, or some other event. Each day before the event, have the children remove one of the rings and count those remaining. Point out that the number left represents the days they will have to wait for the event. For very young children, do not plan to use more than five or six rings.

◆ Children between 4 and 5 years of age can begin to measure time using *arbitrary* measures. Accuracy of measurement does not matter. You are only interested in introducing the idea that time can be measured.

- Give children a stopwatch and have them see how many seconds it takes them to slide down the slide, brake their trikes to a complete stop, or put their boots on.

- Use the stopwatch to find out how long children can hop on one foot, jump rope, blow bubbles through a straw, or hold their breath.

- Use an hourglass to see if children can clean the table, put the blocks away, or get ready to go out to play before all the sand empties into the bottom half. Or if you have a smaller hourglass, see how many times you have to turn it over before children complete a task.

- Have the children use an old kitchen timer to set the number of minutes the bread or cookies they made will bake, or to see if they can complete a puzzle, build a tower, or wash a table before the timer goes off.

- Add clipboards and markers for children to use as they time their activities. The paper on the clipboards might be marked in half, or quarters, or just left plain for children to record marks, or make sketches of their activities. The point is not accuracy of measurement or counting, but rather giving children the opportunities to play as if they were keeping records.

◇ Standard 2. Learning About Past, Present, and Future Time

Children have a vague sense of the passage of time. They understand things happened "a long time ago, before we were here," and they have initial understanding of things that will happen in the future, "When I'm a teenager I'll get a tattoo."

You can foster children's sense of the passage of time by encouraging them to talk about the passage of time, extending and expanding their ability to think in terms of past, present, and future time. In connection with their actual experiences, use every opportunity to use time words. Talk about today, tomorrow, yesterday, this month, next week, this morning, this afternoon, and so on. "This morning we will. . . ." "Tomorrow is the day the firefighters come." "Do you remember, last week we planted potatoes. Whose potato is sprouting?" "Yesterday, we had fun when we peeled apples for our pie."

Children can be asked

- how many days it has been since Alberto's birthday.

- what they liked best about your Halloween celebration that they would like to repeat for Thanksgiving.

- what they can do this month that they could not do last month.

- what they did last week.

- to count the sunny or snowy days during the week, or to count the number of days since the Thanksgiving celebration.

- to tell about what they liked best about the day, what they liked about lunch, or how they felt when walking in the rain.

Take photos of children at work and play. You can mount them in photo albums or just put them on a table. Children will handle them, look at them, and talk about what they did. As they do so, talk about the day the photos were taken, name the day of the week, and name the number of days that have passed since they were taken.

Place photos in small photo books labeling them with children's names and what children were doing at the time. If resources permit, send copies of photo books home with children from time to time. If resources are scarce, take turns sending the book home with children so each family can enjoy it.

Read books to children about the passage of time. Some examples are

Rosemary Wells. (1994). *Night Sounds, Morning Colors.*

This book is divided into four vignettes of the sights and smells that are present in the morning and evening. Ask children what they hear, smell, and see when they first wake up on a beautiful fall day and experience the sun shining through the window like a stream of gold honey. You could take dictation and create your own class book of "Morning Colors," or sounds and sights. Children would illustrate their ideas. Do the same for night sounds, perhaps making a book during the winter, fall, and spring.

Sharon Taberski. (1996). *Morning, Noon and Night: Poems to Fill Your Day.*

This book contains poetry for filling your day. Poems for waking up, on the way to school, and at school help children order the routines of their day. Ask children to pick a favorite time of their day and write or dictate a poem about this time.

Jean Craighead George. (1999). *Morning, Noon, and Night.*

Teachers take photos of children to document historical play.

The day of a raccoon is celebrated. Very young children gain an understanding of the cycle of time as the day passes.

After becoming familiar with the book, 4- and 5-year-olds could create their own time line of the day, illustrating what they do in the morning, at school, at noon, in the afternoon, and in the evening.

◆ Time concepts are also introduced through narrative stories. Narratives generally have a beginning, middle, and an end. Select stories that place events in an order from beginning to end. For instance, you might read or tell the story of:

- *The Three Little Pigs*
- *The Gingerbread Boy*
- *Little Red Riding Hood*
- *The Little Red Hen*

After story reading, ask children some questions. Ask them

- What happened first?
- Then what happened?
- How did the story end?

◆ After children have heard repeated readings or tellings of the same story, have them take part in acting out the stories. Assign children the roles of the three pigs and the wolf and then decide where the pig's houses will be built. To get children started, you will have to act as narrator. Keep the play moving along by saying, "First, the pigs built . . . ," followed by the rest of the story. Children *take turns* acting out their roles, saying the lines of the pigs and the wolf. *Take turns* so most children get a turn at any one play.

The point is for children to learn to sequence events, not just in their day, but in stories as well. To follow-up the experience, ask children to paint, draw, or construct their own pictures of the stories.

◆   After children are acquainted with historical narratives, stories, and myths, they can draw, dictate, or write the stories of their lives. You might give children a large sheet of construction paper folded in half and then in thirds. Label one-third "Before," the next "During," and the last "After." Cut between the panels. Have children draw a picture under the labeled panel of what they do before, during, and after:

  • school

  • Halloween night

  • getting ready to go to bed

  • going on a trip

Or label the panels "Yesterday," "Today," and "Tomorrow," and have children draw something they did in the past, are doing currently, and will do in the future.

◇   **Standard 3. Learning to Record the Changes That Occur with the Passage of Time**

Change results from the passage of time. Change is all around the children. All they have to do is begin observing and recording the changes that occur in themselves and their families.

Changes in Themselves

◆   Measure the children. Cut a strip of paper as long as each child is tall. Put these together to make a graph of the height of children in the class.

Now ask the children to find out how long they were when they were born. Cut another piece of paper (of a different color than the first strip) the same length as each child's birth length. Paste these on top of the first strip. Ask children to compare their height now to their birth length. Why did they change?

◆   Ask children to think about something they wanted in the past but no longer want. Name the thing and perhaps even find a picture of it in a catalog or magazine. Then ask them to think of something they want today. Find a picture of that. Finally, ask them to name and find a picture of something they think they'll want when they are teenagers. Fold a piece of large construction paper in thirds. Label the thirds as "Wanted," "Want," and "Will Want." Have children place their pictures in the appropriate columns. Discuss why their wants have changed and will continue to change.

◆   Keep a portfolio of each child's work. Date the work and samples included in the portfolio. Set aside time to review the portfolios with each child in the middle of the school year and at the end. Ask the children to think of the things they can do now, or have learned, that they could not do or did not know at the beginning of the school year. You could make a class booklet of "Things We Have Learned in Preschool."

Changes in Their Families

◆   Do children know their parents were once just as old as they are now? Ask parents to send photographs of themselves when they were about their children's ages. Take individual photographs of the children. Make a bulletin board of the photos, placing each child's photo with that of his or her parents as children. Talk about the changes that have occurred in their parents.

◆   Take advantage of naturally occurring changes in children's families such as the birth of a baby. When a baby is old enough, ask the parents to bring him or her to class. Before the baby comes, teach the children some baby songs to sing to their visitor, such as T. Glazer's "Eye Winker, Tom Tinker, Chin Chopper." *The Complete Book of Rhymes, Songs, Poems, Finger Plays and Chants* by Shiller, Silberg, and Wright is a good source of finger plays. *Hush Songs: African American Lullabies* by Joyce Carol Thomas is another good choice.

◆   While children are choosing which songs to sing to the baby, ask them to list their own favorite songs. Discuss how these differ from the baby songs they have chosen to sing to the new baby.
      After the baby has visited, read P. Hutchins' *You'll Soon Grow into Them,* the story of Titch, who grows out of his clothes and gets hand-me-downs. Display some baby clothes on the library table along with books about babies and growing up. Let the children handle the clothes. They may try to put them on. The point is to let children explore the idea that they have grown and changed since they were babies.

◆   When a child in the class will be moving, read Angela Johnson's *The Leaving Morning,* the story of a family moving and saying good-bye to all of their friends and their apartment. The class can make a "Good-bye" book for the child who is moving, and he or she can make a "Good-bye" book for the class. Children can draw, dictate, or write the story of their pictures for the book.

◆   Tomie dePaola's *Nana Upstairs, Nana Downstairs* is a fine story to read should a child lose a grandparent. It conveys the idea that even though a grandparent or an older relative has died, that person will come back in your memory whenever you think of him or her.

◆   *Tell Me a Story Mama*, written by Angela Johnson and illustrated by David Soman, tells the story of a young girl and her mother remembering Mama's childhood memories. It puts children in touch with the lives of their parents.

◆   Follow the reading by requesting children's parents to tell stories of their own childhood to their children. Ask parents to write these stories out so you can read them to the class and make your own book of Our Families' Stories. See tear out page 80.

Changes in the Others, the Classroom, and the Neighborhood

◆   Do the children know you were once a baby? Ask the teachers and staff to bring photos of themselves when they were babies and adults. Put these on a bulletin board. Label the baby pictures with a number and those of adults with their names. Label the board "Which Baby Is Your Teacher?" Attach an answer book with a string to the board.
      There will be no need to prompt discussion about change and growth. Children, staff, parents, and other visitors will be drawn to the board as they try to figure out which baby is a particular teacher or other staff person.

◆ Read P. Parnall's *The Apple Tree.* Then observe the changes that occur in a tree on the school grounds or in the neighborhood. Write your own story of "Our Tree."

◆ Read Virginia Lee Burton's classic *Little House,* the story of how a city grows up around a house. After reading the story, take a walk around your school to find houses that are being repainted, repaired, or changed in some way. Take photos of changes, such as new neighbors moving in, a house being built, an apartment building being renovated, or the street being repaired. Make a chart of changes in your neighborhood with the pictures. Five-year-olds can keep a record of these changes by marking them on a calendar or drawing pictures in a book titled *Our Neighborhood.*

◆ Read Sharon Dennis Wyeth's *Something Beautiful,* the story of a child searching for something beautiful in her neighborhood. She sees a jump rope, beads, smooth pocket stones, and other happy things. After you read the book, take another walk through the school or surrounding neighborhood to find new beautiful things. Children can record their findings on clipboards or through photos.

◇ **Standard 4. Using the Methods of the Historian: Observing, Collecting Data, Reflecting, and Reaching Conclusions**

◆ Begin with photographs of children when they were babies. Ask them to describe what life was like for them when they were so young. They may want to collect additional information by asking their parents or other relatives to tell them stories of when they were little.

   Then read A. A. Milne's poem, "The End." It begins, "When I was one, I was just begun; When I was two, I was barely new." Have children reach conclusions about their past by making a booklet of the poem. They can draw a picture of when they were 1, 2, 3, 4, and 5 years old and then when they will be 6 years old. One teacher had the children make a mural of the poem as a door covering.

Fossils and arrowheads bring the past to life for young children.

◆ Obtain artifacts from the past from a local museum, junk shop, or your home. Place the artifacts on a table and let children observe, experiment, with and explore these. The artifacts might be as simple as a hand-turned pencil sharpener, small handheld sharpeners, and an electric sharpener. As children sharpen pencils they discover which sharpener is fastest, or most efficient. Listen to children talk about their experiences, such as "Children used this sharpener a long time ago," and build on them. Record children's comments and conclusions.

◆ You might bring to class an old hand eggbeater, a ball-bearing beater, and an electric beater. Have the children try to whip egg whites using each one of the beaters. Collect data by recording the time it takes for the egg whites to hold their shape with each of the beaters. Ask, "Which beater is best?" "Why?" "How are the beaters different?" Draw conclusions by having children vote on the beater they would choose.

When you are finished, add a small amount of sugar and some coconut or nuts and raisins to the egg whites and bake them in a slow oven for healthy macaroons.

◆ If you can, find old toys, such as jackdaws. Show children how children used to play with these toys. Observe what children do with the toys and how they compare them to their own toys.

◆ Read Sally M. Walker's *The 18 Penny Goose,* a story of family life during the late 1700s. Have children compare life today to that of the 1700s. Have children discuss how life differs today from in the past. Ask them the following:

- Where does the story take place?

- When did it take place?

- Do people and things change throughout the story?

- What in the book gives us clues as to the time and place of the story?

- What is the same today as it was when Letty was a child?

- How are our clothes the same as Letty's? How are they different?

- What food did Letty eat? What foods do we eat?

- How do our homes differ? How are they alike?

Have children draw conclusions about life long ago by asking them why they would or would not want to have lived when Letty did.

◆ Nearly every community has a living history museum or nearby historic site. Take a field trip to the site. While you are there, interview the guides and look at records and artifacts of the past.

Reflect on your experiences at the site. Ask children to pretend they lived during that time and to draw a picture of themselves as if they had.

◇ **Reflecting and Reaching Conclusions**

Children can reflect on their experiences by organizing and communicating their year in school through a time line and booklet.

◆ Make a time line of the year in preschool so children will be able to reflect on their own past. Start at the beginning of the year by keeping track of events of the day, week, and month on a large calendar. Calendars are not useful when children are drilled on the days of the week, the letters of the days of the week, and so on. Calendars are useful, however, to keep track of time and the events of the school. For example, you could

- Put a photo of each child on the day of his or her birthday.

- Draw a picture of a butterfly or write a note to mark the day the butterfly emerged from the chrysalis.

- Mark the day you visited the fire station with a picture or photograph of the children at the station.

◆ Find a place to display the calendars. If you do not have room in a coatroom, hallway, or bathroom, you could start a booklet of calendars. What you want is for children to be able to review their time in the preschool. One teacher hung each month's calendar in a coatroom and found the children frequently talking about the events of the past.

◆ At the end of the year write, draw, or dictate a history book of the year. It could be titled *Our Year in Kindergarten.* Each child thinks of the event or experience that was personally special or most enjoyable. Then the child draws a picture and writes or dictates a description of the event. These drawings are put together in a class book. Some teachers have found that they can photocopy the individual pages to make a copy of the book for each child to take home.

◇ **Extending and Expanding to the Early Primary Grades**

Primary children can do all of the following:

◆ Interview their parents to find out what their lives were like and write books about *When Mother Was Young, When I Was Young,* or *When My Grandmother Was Young.*

◆ Learn to tell time using conventional measures such as the clock and calendar. Ask them to keep a diary of their life at school, illustrating it with pictures. At the end of a semester, ask them to reach conclusions about their life at school by listing the five things they like best about their life and five things they learned.

◆ Make a time line of their lives. Using photos from home, drawings, or magazine pictures, they can record the events of their lives on long mural paper or in an album.

◆ Study the history of your school. Have children find out who named the school and why. What was on the land before the school was built? How has the school changed since it was built? The children will need to look at old records and photographs, or go to a city or county office to look at records of the past.

◆ Read stories of courage. These might include

Allen Jay and the Underground Railroad by M. Targ Brill

Across the Wide Dark Sea: The Mayflower Journey by J. Van Leeuwen

Days of Courage: The Little Rock Story by R. Kelso

Seven Brave Women by B. Hearne and B. Andersen

Ask children to put themselves in the shoes of the lead characters. Ask how they felt, why they were so courageous, and what they would do in similar circumstances. What were the hopes, fears, motives, strengths, and weaknesses of the characters?

Ask children to read these books to each other. They could take turns reading two or three pages or a chapter to each other.

◆ Primary children are ready to learn about others in place and time. These books, recommended by the National Children's Book Council, offer children images and stories of children of different cultures and heritages:

Native American

Native American Life by Jill Foran

Buffalo Before Breakfast by Mary Pope Osborne

Legend of the Bluebonnets by Tomie de Paola

African American

In Daddy's Arms I Am Tall by Javaka Steptoe

Song of the Trees by Mildred D. Taylor

Langston's Train Ride by Robert Burleigh

Other

The House in the Mail by Rosemary and Tom Wells

Heading for Better Times by Duane Damon

◆ Conduct an oral history. Children can

- select a subject, perhaps an older relative or neighbor.
- do some research about the life of the person they will interview. They could read books about the time the person lived or become familiar with the home-town, state, or country the person lived in.
- decide on what they want to find out when they interview the person.
- record the person's story using a tape recorder or through writing.
- reach conclusions about the person and his or her life.

◇ Documenting Children's Learning

Document children's historical knowledge with a web.

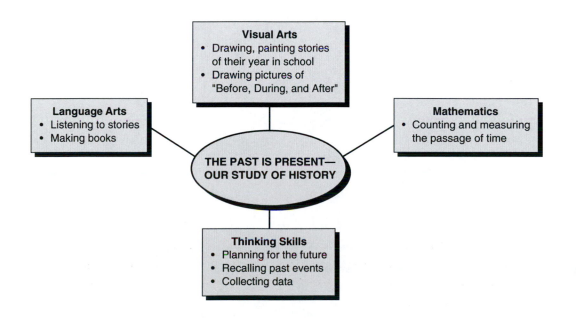

Date _____

Dear Parents:

Because we want children to develop a sense of the past, your children will be asking you for a number of things. During the next month or so, your child will ask you to tell stories about his or her life as a baby and toddler, as well as stories about when you were a child.

Children will like to hear about their favorite toys, what they played and ate, and who their friends were. They will like stories of when they said their first word and what it was. Show them photos of when they were little, and talk about how much they have changed since they first were born.

Children also like to hear stories about the long, long ago when you were little. Tell them about your favorite clothing, the things you did that were scary or fun, or what you liked best about your preschool experience. You might teach them one of the games you played as a child or bake your favorite cookies, bread, or other special food.

Later in the year we will be asking you to send photographs of yourself as a baby and today, and photographs of your children when they were babies.

We will be asking children to record their ideas about the past. You will enjoy the booklets and pictures the children will bring home with them about the past.

Sincerely,

Time Words—Observation

Date	Center/Area	Children	Time Words Used	Accuracy		
				Not at all	Some	Accurate

81

Measuring Time—Observation

Date	Center/Area	Children	Measuring Time (Record How, Why)

Methods of the Historian—Observation

Date	Center/Area	Children	Identifying Problems	Collecting Information	Reaching Conclusions

History Concepts

Interview children and record their responses to the following questions:

1. Tell about something you liked or remember that happened a long time ago; something that happened to you this week; and something you think will happen when you are older.

2. What has changed since you first came to school? What have you learned? What can you do now that you could not do then? What will you learn?

Analyze children's responses for

- completeness

- accuracy

- number of details

7

Earth: The Place We Live

FOR THE TEACHER

◇ What You'll Need to Know

Children's ideas of the earth are dominated by artificialistic thought. Children believe the earth and the things on it were made for their own use and purpose, or they think someone else made the earth. One child explained, "The mountains made themselves"; another said, "My daddy made the beach so we can go swimming."

Likewise, children will not be able to understand the concept that their earth is a part of a solar system until they are nearly preadolescents. Nevertheless, during the period of early childhood, children can be introduced to the idea of the earth's rotation on its axis and around the sun, as well as the concepts of atmosphere and its effects on life. This introduction, however, should build an initial awareness that the earth, the place we live, is part of a larger solar system, and that this system affects our lives on earth.

Children's primitive ideas of the earth they live on, however, do not keep children from acting as true geographers. They dig in the earth, explore the nature of water, let sand sift through their fingers, and question "Why?" From these initial sensory and exploratory experiences in their own home and school yard, children learn that the earth, the place they live, is covered with different surfaces, and they become acquainted with different landforms, bodies of water, soils, and plant and animal life.

Children's spontaneous and everyday concepts of their earth can be expanded and extended in the preschool. Children are taught to identify and name landforms and bodies of water in their environment. By 4 or 5 years of age, most children will have traveled, read books, and watched videos, movies, and television, thereby gaining vicarious ideas about the nature of the earth far from them.

◇ Geography Standards: Key Concepts

The geography standards include the concepts that:

- The earth is a part of the solar system.

- The earth is covered with a variety of surfaces.

- Each place has characteristics that make it special.

- A wide variety of plants and animals live on the earth.

◇ Goals and Objectives

Children will be able to talk about how the sun and moon affect their lives.

Children will be able to identify and name two surfaces in their play yard or neighborhood.

Children will identify animal and plant life common to their area as well as plants and animals that live in different parts of the earth.

Children's drawings, paintings, constructions, and sand and water play will include and reflect the landforms, bodies of water, plants, animals, and architecture that make their place unique and special.

◇ What You'll Need

A Laboratory

Your laboratory is the school yard, school, and children's neighborhood. Each place, just like each child, will be different. No two school yards or neighborhoods are alike. Take a walk around your play yard and through the neighborhood to observe the things that make these spaces special.

Venture farther away from the school to determine whether there are specific bodies of water, landforms, or other areas near the school or children's homes that could be used as a part of your geographic laboratory. Make a list of the things you see and the words that can be used to describe them. By doing so, you will be ready to focus children's observations on salient things in their environment and quickly give them the words they need to organize these things.

Sand and Water Tables

In addition to the immediate environment, you will find sand and water tables useful. Out-of-doors, even a small pile of clean sand can fill the need. You will need to make certain the sand is covered when not in use. Indoors, you can use purchased sand tables, or you can use a discarded wading pool, a plastic dishpan, or a large box lid as a sand table (see Chapter 2).

Outdoors, any small, shallow container of water will do. Indoors, it is a little harder to arrange for water play. Teachers may cover tables and the surrounding areas with

Children experiment to determine which things grow in the soil.

SAND AND WATER FOR CHILDREN WITH SPECIAL NEEDS

Children with special needs, especially those who do not have the opportunity to crawl, sit, or stand on the earth, learn from water and sand play. Such tactile play, along with your words describing their actions, helps visually impaired children establish concepts of water and earth. Children with hearing impairments develop concepts when you talk or sign to them about what they are doing. Emphasize their visual observations.

For children who cannot get down on the ground to play in sand or water, bring it to them. Put a small sandbox and container of water on a table they can use so they, too, can experience the surfaces of the earth.

---

plastic cloths and place plastic dishpans half-filled with water on tables. Others find using sinks in the room for water play satisfactory, or use small wading pools for special water explorations (see Chapter 2).

You will also need

- magnifying glasses

- small trowels for children to dig with

- plastic buckets

- scales (See Figure 7.1 to make a coat hanger scale.)

- a clear plastic bottle for each child

- drawing tools, mural paper, and other papers

Children's Books

You will find a variety of books useful. Adult photography books of children's immediate environment or of places far from them, reference books about oceans and rivers, as

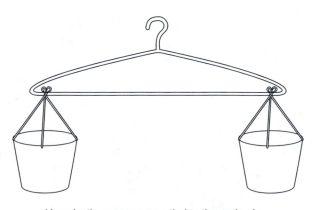

Use plastic or paper cups tied to the ends of a plastic coat hanger.

FIGURE 7.1
A Coat Hanger Scale

well as picture books, books of poetry, and fantasy stories serve to extend and expand children's experiences with their earth.

Baylor, B. (1974). *Everybody loves a rock.* New York: Aladin.

dePaola, T. (1988). *Legend of the Indian paintbrush.* New York: Putnam Publishing Group Junior.

English, K. (1996). *Neeny coming, Neeny going.* Mahwah, NJ: Bridge Water.

Ets, M. H. (1955). *Play with me.* New York: Viking.

Fleming, D. (1991). *In the tall, tall grass.* New York: Holt.

Fleming, D. (1993). *In the small, small pond.* New York: Holt.

Gans, R. (1986). *Rock collecting.* New York: HarperCollins.

Garelick, M., & Garrison, B. (1996). *Look at the moon.* New York: Mondo Publishing Co.

McCloskey, R. (1948). *Blueberries for Sal.* New York: Viking.

McCloskey, R. (1952). *One morning in Maine.* New York: Viking.

Other Resources

Your Big Back Yard is a magazine chock-full of resources and ideas for children's geography learning. Subscriptions can be ordered from:

National Wildlife Federation
11100 Wildlife Center Drive
Reston, VA 20190-5362
1-800-822-9919
www.nwf.org

The Home-School Connection

Involve parents as partners in their children's education. Ask them to help you reinforce concepts key to the study of geography in their home. You might use the tear out sheets at the end of this chapter (pages 101–102, 104–105). These sheets invite parents to

- introduce children to the names and types of landforms near to them as well as those that are far away

- be involved in children's learning about the surfaces that cover the earth

- enjoy and value the work their children have completed

◇ Evaluating and Assessing Children's Learning

Show children pictures of the surfaces of the earth in the school yard and neighborhood. Ask each child to identify and name two surfaces in their play yard or neighborhood.

Show children photographs or pictures of plants and animals common to your area. Ask each child to name and identify three plants and two animals. Ask what other plants and animals they know and list these.

Show children photographs or pictures of various landforms present in your area. Ask children to name these.

Record children's answers using the tear out sheet on page 100. Forward these to children's parents with the letter found on the tear out sheet on page 101 at the end of this chapter.

─────────────── **FOR THE CHILDREN** ───────────────

◇ **Standard 1. The Earth Is a Part of the Solar System**

As the earth rotates around the sun, children can note the changes that occur during the day. Never ask children to look directly at the sun, but rather to observe, experience, and record the effects of the sun.

◆ Conduct some *experiments* with the sun. On a sunny day, give children buckets of water and large paint brushes. Have them paint everything in sight. As they do so, ask them to notice which places dry the quickest. Ask:

- Which places are in the sun?

- Which places are in the shade?

- What do you think happened?

◆ On another sunny day when the children have painted everything in sight, make a record of their observations. Give them clipboards containing sheets with the headings Sun—Dry and Shade—Damp so they can record their findings by drawing a picture of the things that were dry in the sun and damp in the shade.

◆ Wash doll clothes and doll bedding, towels, and other clothes. Hang some in the sun and some in the shade to dry so you can talk about where things dry the fastest and why.

◆ What do you wear on a hot and sunny day? What do you wear on a cold and rainy day? On another hot and sunny day make scrapbooks of clothes children would like to wear on a hot and sunny day. Tear pictures of swimsuits, shorts, halter tops, sun dresses, sun hats, and other sunny day clothes. Follow-up by making another scrapbook of clothes they might wear if they lived where it was very cold all of the time.

◆ Focusing on the night sky is more difficult. But you can use the pictures children drew of the night sky with their parents to start discussions and a study of the night sky.

◆ When children bring their drawings of the shape of the moon to class, mount them on poster board and talk about how the shape of the moon changes. You can tell children that the changes of the moon are related to the rotation of the earth around the sun. Show them pictures of the moon in an encyclopedia or other reference book, but do not try to show them a model of the earth, sun, moon, and stars. These initial experiences will enable them to better understand such a model when they are 11 or 12 years old and think abstractly.

◆ Sometimes conditions are such that you can see a daytime moon in the sky in the morning or late afternoon. When you and the children see the moon in the daytime, you could teach them the rhyme,

> *Little day moon is a toy balloon*

> *Lost by a child in her play*

◆ Ask children what shape the day moon is. Make a picture of the shape of the day moon. Then ask children to observe the moon that night and bring to school a picture of the moon they see. Point out that the shape of the moon is the same when you can see it during the day as it is at night.

Read the Mother Goose rhyme

"Bedtime"

> *The Man in the Moon looked out of the moon,*
>
> *Looked out of the moon and said,*
>
> *"Tis time for all children on the earth*
>
> *to think about getting to bed."*

Read May Garelick and Barbara Garrison's *Look at the Moon,* the story of a girl who wonders if everyone sees the same moon. The watercolor gouaches and collages illustrating the book can motivate children to make their own moon book. Start by talking about things the children and their parents do at night. Then give children painting materials, along with strips of paper and fabric, and have them each draw or paint a picture to place in their class book about the moon.

Read Leland Jacob's *Good Night, Mr. Beetle.* The book ends with the refrain, "I'll see you in the morning, when the sun comes up." Tell them that this is what one mother said to her child before bedtime and ask children what their parents say when they tuck them into bed at night. Record children's responses on a chart titled "When I Go to Bed."

Sing "Twinkle, twinkle, little star, how I wonder what you are. Way up in the world so high, like a diamond in the sky."

◆ Ask children what they think the stars are, and record their answers on an experience chart. Some children may draw their ideas on the chart as well.

Sing "Twinkle, twinkle, little moon, won't you shine into my room," or "Twinkle, twinkle, little light, how you make our room so bright."

What else do children see that twinkles? Ask them to make up their own twinkle rhyme.

◆ Play the riddle

> A STAR
>
> BIGGER THAN A HOUSE, HIGHER THAN A TREE
>
> *Oh, whatever can that be?*

Write children's answers on a chart, and have them decorate the chart with drawings.

◇ Standard 2. The Earth Is Covered with Different Surfaces

Take walking field trips. Bring a camera with you so children can look at photographs of their trip later and reflect on their experiences.

- As you walk, point out and name the surfaces covering the earth: "The ground is soft," "This concrete was made by humans and is very hard," "The sand feels bumpy under our feet." These experiences build children's awareness of the fact that the earth on which they live is covered with different surfaces, some of which have been made by humans.

- On another trip ask children to count and name the different surfaces they encounter. Discuss the surfaces. Which are hard? Soft? Firm? What would happen if they dropped something on a hard surface? What would happen if they fell on a hard surface?

  Which surface is easiest to walk or ride on? Ask children why they think this is so. Have children take turns walking or running on different surfaces and stop on a given signal. Or they could ride their trikes on the surfaces and try to stop these on a given signal. Talk with them about the differences between soft, slick, smooth, and hard surfaces and how these affect their safety when walking or riding wheel toys.

  Keep a record of children's findings. You can make a chart or take photographs of the children exploring the different surfaces. Label these and make a poster titled "Surfaces on Our Earth."

- Take another trip. This day walk a little farther from the school. Ask the children to note the different types of soil they see. You could divide the children into groups of three or four, with an adult volunteer for each group. Give each group an assignment card with directions and a space for recording findings.

  Note the kinds of homes. Do people live in apartment buildings, high-rise buildings, duplexes, single-family homes, trailers, or on farms? What architectural features do you see? Are there wraparound porches, shutters, gables, stairs? What is the style of architecture? What industries, farms, businesses, churches and synagogues, and stores are in the neighborhood? Observe the surfaces children will encounter. Is there grass? A place children can dig? Are some surfaces covered with human-made materials? What plants and animals are found on the play yard? How many trees are there?

  Direct the small groups to:

  find out what color the soil is where plants are growing

  note the color of soil where no plants are growing

  collect soil samples in small plastic bags for examination once back in the classroom

  look for footprints in the soil or sand or on the sidewalk surface

  record what different types of soil feel like

◆ Sand play can take place any day. If children are to build with sand, however, you need to add a water source. Half-filled plastic squirt bottles are useful in building and limit how wet children can get. After children have explored the sand, you might do the following:

  - Have children fill two containers that are exactly the same with sand. Using a coat hanger scale (see Figure 7.1), have children weigh the two containers. Next have them add water to one of the containers, and then weigh both again. What happened?

  - Ask children to dry "sand cakes" in the sun and shade to find which will dry the quickest.

  - Provide small wooden or plastic animals to promote dramatic play.

- Give children an old plastic dishpan they can fill with water to make a lake or pond.

- Add wheel toys, cars, trucks, and cranes to the sand area, and assign the task of making roads for them out of sand.

◆ For this activity you will need permission to dig in the play yard or school grounds, adult volunteers, magnifying glasses, and a container for dirt. Mark off a 12″ square in the yard. If there is grass or hard soil, you will have to begin the digging, but ask children to help dig a hole 12 inches square by 6 inches deep with their small trowels. Tell them they are like geographers who want to find out what soil is and what they can find in the soil.

As you and the children dig, note the different colors of soil. The top layer should be darkest, and you should be able to identify roots as you dig. Have children place the soil in a box lid and return to the classroom.

- Divide the class into committees of three or four with an adult volunteer for each small group. Cover the tables with newspapers, and give each group a portion of the soil.

- Ask children and the volunteers to use their magnifying glasses to find

  grains of sand in the soil

  plant leaves, stems, roots

  larvae or pupae of insects

  adult insects, earthworms, or spiders

- Provide paper and markers for children to draw or write about the things they find in the soil.

◆ After you've discussed and compared the findings of each group, return the soil to the play yard, carefully recovering the area to leave it as you originally found it.

  Investigate different aspects of soil.

- Find out what lives in the soil of the earth. Turn over some rocks and identify the animals and insects living under each. Five-year-olds could draw a map of where the insects and animals were when the rock was first turned over.

- Collect a variety of soils. You might use the letter to parents on page 102 asking them to send a small sample of soil from their yard or neighborhood. Children may bring in soil that is sandy, loamy, or clayey.

- Experiment with the soil. This will be messy, so cover the table with plastic or paper. Arrange for children to test different soils by placing a sample of each in a cup of water and observing what happens to the soil.

  How long does it take for the soil to settle on the bottom?

  Which soils change color?

  Which change the color of the water?

  Give each child a small clipboard, a marker, and a paper to record his or her findings. The goal is to have children play with soil and water and to find out how different soils feel and behave in water, not necessarily to develop profound hypotheses. Still, you will want to talk with children about their experiments. (Use the tear out sheet on page 103, and ask children to record their findings with an X or a check mark.)

◆   Children love to collect and play with stones. Perhaps they feel good in their hands or are just fun to pick up and look at. You can use children's innate interest in rocks to foster categorization. Make or obtain a sorting box (see Figure 7.2).

• Give 3- and 4-year-olds plastic containers and rocks. They'll fill the containers with rocks, spill them out, and begin again. This spill-and-fill activity builds the beginning awareness of the physical properties of rocks, as well as our earth. As they play, you can ask them to describe how different rocks feel and what colors and shapes they are. Or you can describe the rocks to the children.

◇ Standard 3. Each Place Has Unique Characteristics

◆   Identify the major bodies of water and landforms that make your place special. Ask parents to take their children to see these and to name the rivers, lakes, ponds, hills, or mountains for their children. (See the tear out sheet on page 101 at the end of this chapter.)

◆   Take the children to see the prominent landform in your area. Then do a class mural. If you live near a desert, the mural could be titled "In Our Large, Large Desert," or if near a mountain, "In the Beautiful Mountain," and so on (see Figure 7.3).

◆   If you live in a city, you may want to take a trip to look at the different types of buildings and the ways people travel, and make a mural called "In Our Large, Large City."

◆   If it is not possible for children to experience spaces that make their neighborhood and community special, you could view videos, movies, and photographs and read books about these places together.

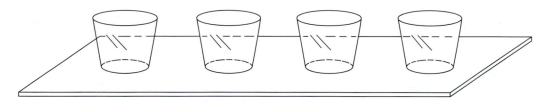

Glue clear plastic cups to a board.

FIGURE 7.2
A Sorting Box

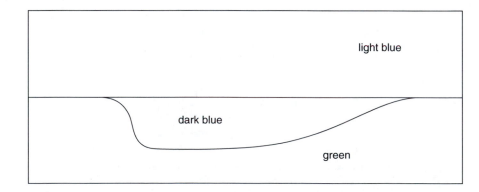

FIGURE 7.3
Our Small, Small Pond Mural

◆ Try to personalize these vicarious experiences. You might do the following:

- Talk about and show pictures of the places where children were born, have lived, or will be moving to. Their parents may be able to share photographs or videos of these places.

- When you eat oranges, apples, pineapples, blueberries, or other foods, find out where they were grown. Show children the place on a map and pictures of apple or orange orchards. Find out what foods are raised in the place you live.

- Sing songs about different places. Children enjoy learning "This Land Is Your Land" and the opening phrases of "America, the Beautiful."

◇ **Standard 4. A Wide Variety of Plants and Animals Live on the Earth**

◆ You can start by taking a walk to identify the things that live and grow in the soil on the play yard or around the school. Even in a crowded city, children can find and identify plants growing in the cracks of the sidewalk or curbs and observe a variety of birds.

- You could ask children who have walked the yard and neighborhood frequently

  to find the three most common birds, name these, and draw them in their journals

  to list the three most common plants growing in cracks in the sidewalk, and draw these in their journals

◆ Read Marie Hall Ets' *Play with Me* (1955), the story of a girl learning to be quiet with shy woodland creatures. Then ask children to sit or stand very still in a field, on a park bench, or on a bench along a busy city street and wait for birds and other animals to show themselves. Have children record their findings or write or dictate their own book, *Sit with Me.*

◆ Show children how to make viewing tubes to take on their walks. Looking through a viewing tube helps children focus their observations on the details in their environment. Binoculars are difficult for young children to learn to use, but after they become used to a viewing tube, they can generally learn to use a telescope (see Figure 7.4).

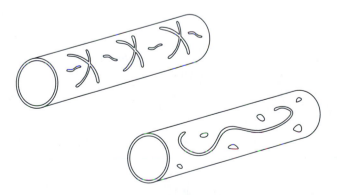

Use toilet paper or paper towel tubes decorated by the children.

FIGURE 7.4
A Viewing Tube

◆ If you can, take a riding field trip to a special lake, pond, or swamp. Make sure children and their parents understand the purpose for the trip. The purpose may be to note the plants and birds that make their home in the tall grass, or to collect pond water to look at under a magnifying glass back in the classroom. Taking photographs of children as they explore the environment enables them to recall and reflect on their experience later.

◆ After your trip, read D. Fleming's *In the Small, Small Pond* (1993). Make a class mural titled "In the Small, Small Pond." Give children sponges and pans of blue, green, and white paint. On a large sheet of poster paper, they can sponge in the grass, pond, and sky. While the paper dries, they can draw one plant, animal, or other thing they observed in or near the pond or in the sky. Hang the poster in a hallway with a sign telling about the trip to document children's learning (see Figure 7.3).

◇ **Reflecting**

Have children organize their experiences. Provide them with a table so they can display their rock collection or the things they found in the soil. Have pictures and books ready to add to the collection or the soil samples. Hang pictures children have drawn and place stories they've written near the table.

◇ **Extending and Expanding to the Early Primary Grades**

Children in the primary grades can do the following:

◆ Start a rock collection. Children can find and collect rocks on their walks. You can bring rocks to the classroom, or ask children's parents to help you start a rock collection.

By 6 years of age or so, children can sort rocks on the basis of one or more categories, putting all the red, smooth stones in one container and the hard, gray stones in another.

◆ Read Roma Gans' *Rock Collecting* (1986) and Brad Baylor's *Everybody Loves a Rock* (1974). Start naming the types of rocks the children encounter. Just as children love to impress the adults and older siblings around them by naming the dinosaurs, so will they enjoy knowing and using the names of rocks. They find it a source of

---

TIME TO PRETEND

After you read the following books or poems to children, stir their imaginations and ask them to draw, paint, or build.

- Read any of Beatrix Potter's tales of Peter Rabbit and his friends and draw their neighborhood.

- Read *Brown Bear, Brown Bear What Do You See?* and *Polar Bear, Polar Bear What Do You Hear?*, both written by Bill Martin, Jr., and illustrated by Eric Carle, and draw Brown Bear's and Polar Bear's neighborhoods. How are their neighborhoods alike and how are they different?

- Read "Hey Diddle Diddle," and have children draw, paint, or construct the cat, cow, and fiddle's neighborhood.

Children collect different kinds of rocks by the river.

pleasure to say to their parents, grandparents, and older siblings, "Yes, this rock is sedimentary. You can tell because I can make it into sand just by rubbing it."

◆ Read stories of other places. Just a few examples are *One Morning in Maine* (1952) or *Blueberries for Sal* (1998) by Robert McCloskey; *Neeny Coming, Neeny Going* (1996) by Karen English, the story of life on Daufskie Island, one of South Carolina's Sea Islands; and *The Legend of the Indian Paintbrush* (1988) by Tomie dePaola.

Ask children to compare the place they live with the places described in the stories. How are landforms and bodies of water similar and how do they differ? Now children can be introduced to a variety of factual books about geography. You could provide them with books featuring the geography of Maine, South Carolina, and the West so they can compare the story descriptions with factual information.

◇ Documenting Children's Learning

To document children's learning, you could do the following activities:

◆ Compile a photograph album of 3-year-olds' adventures with their world. You could include photos of children playing in water and sand or on a walking field trip. Send the book to each child's home along with the tear out sheet letter on page 105.

◆ Have older children make a quilt of the things they've observed on the earth. First talk about the things they've experienced—the different surfaces, soils, architecture, plants, and animals they've observed. Ask each child to think of some special thing they've learned and draw it with fabric markers on a square piece of cloth. Assemble the squares and hang the "quilt," along with the sign "Things We've Learned About Our Earth," in a place where parents, other children, and teachers can enjoy it (see Figure 7.5).

Figure 7.5
Our Earth Quilt

Make a web documenting the integrated learning that took place while studying the earth.

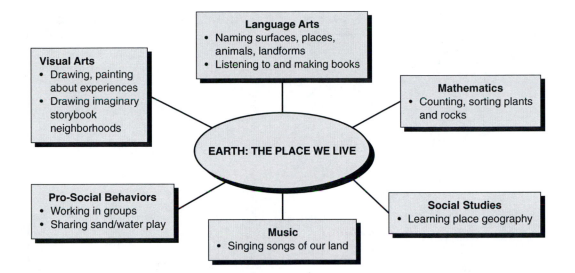

Earth: The Place We Live					
Name	Date	Surfaces	Plants	Animals	Landforms

Date _____

Dear Parents:

This year we are introducing your children to geographic ideas. One of the ideas we are working on is that each place on earth is unique and different. We started teaching this idea by observing the things in our neighborhood. Now we want children to know that there are other places that may be different from the place we live. You can help by doing the following:

- Read magazines and newspapers with your children and show them pictures or photographs of different landforms—mountains and valleys, streams, waterfalls, deserts, or tropical forests.

- Show children photographs and videos of places you've visited or lived. Talk about what the place was like and how people lived there.

- When you take a trip, name the rivers you cross and the lakes you see and point out landforms.

Thank you for helping your children learn about geography.

Sincerely,

Permission is granted by the publisher to reproduce this page.

101

Date _____

Dear Parents:

As a part of our study of geography, we are observing the soil that makes up our earth. Would you fill the plastic bag attached to this letter with about a half a cup of soil from your yard or neighborhood?

We will sort the soils by color and type, and experiment with them. Your child will bring home a record of these experiments and tell you what we found.

Thank you for your continuing interest in our study of geography.

Sincerely,

Form for Soil Experiment Clipboard

Name   Date

Soil	Dissolves	Settles	Stays the Same
sandy soil			
loamy soil			
clayey soil			
play yard soil			

Date _____

Dear Parents:

Will you help us teach your children that each place on our earth is unique? As you take trips or drive around different areas and places,

- identify the major landforms that make the place special

- name the rivers, lakes, and ponds you see

- talk about going up and down hills, or name the mountains you see in the distance

- talk with your children about the characteristics of different places. If you see a desert, mountain, or swamp, point out what makes each unique.

We appreciate being partners with you in your children's education.

Sincerely,

Date _____

Dear Parents:

Please enjoy this photo album of the things we've learned about geography this past month. Ask your child to tell you about the pictures and the things she or he learned.

Please return the book with your child tomorrow so we can send it to each family.

Sincerely,

Mapping for Young Children

─────────────── **FOR THE TEACHER** ───────────────

◇ **What You'll Need to Know**

A map is a picture of part or all of the earth. We use maps to position ourselves in space. Maps are among the most abstract of tools we use. For children who are in Piaget's concrete operations stage of development, the abstractions of maps are truly beyond their comprehension. Not until children are around 11 or 12 years old can they comprehend the abstractions involved in reading maps.

Nevertheless, it is during the early years that children become aware of maps and how to use them. If children have the opportunity to play with and see maps being used, they will often spontaneously draw or paint their own maps. These maps, of course, are not conventional; they may be as simple and primitive as lines drawn in the sand box "so the trucks know where to go." Children spontaneously make maps as they play with blocks. They may draw a design, calling it the map of the airport they've just built. Other children spontaneously draw and paint maps. One girl painted an elaborate map of a woods, calling it "Little Red Ridinghood's map."

Through informal play with maps, and actually using maps in their daily activities, children do become aware of maps and their use. Understandably, these early experiences with and understanding of maps are embryonic; nevertheless, they are critical because they form the foundation on which later abstract learning can be built.

◇ **Mapping Standards**

The standards include the following concepts:

• **Maps:** Maps, which are themselves symbols, use lines, color, and other symbols to represent reality and are used to locate oneself in space.

• **Scale:** A map is a small picture of a much larger place.

A child spontaneously draws a map to represent her world.

- **Perspective:** A map is a picture of a place as if you were looking at it from above, like a bird in the sky.

◇ **Goals and Objectives**

Children will be able to point to lines representing streets on a class map, identify blue on a map as representing water, and identify other symbols such as railroad tracks, hospitals, and schools, but only if they have seen these things and then found the corresponding symbols on a map.

Children will play with maps, using them as they take pretend trips; tell what a map is used for; follow a map as they take a walking field trip; and use a map to find an object in their room or in the play yard.

Children will draw and build maps as they play.

Children will be able to draw an object from a bird's-eye view.

◇ **What You'll Need**

Concepts of maps and how they are used will be developed over the entire year. Integrated into the total curriculum, children's experiences with maps must be continuous. Some of the experiences may be repeated over weeks and months; others, such as building maps with blocks, will be available on a daily basis.

Maps

You'll need all kinds of maps. Try to find small maps of your area that use a lot of pictures and other symbols. You could contact the following for materials:

- State and local tourist agencies and your local chamber of commerce. These agencies usually publish walking tour maps or guidebooks of the area.

- Local government offices, especially those dealing with public transportation such as the Department of Transportation.

- Local businesses such as rental car companies.

- The National Geographic Society, which offers a free raised globe and other inexpensive maps. The Federal Government Printing Office has hundreds of maps. You may have to pay for some and allow time for delivery. Write or e-mail for a catalog.

You may also print maps from the Internet using Map Quest or another mapping website. These can be specific to the places you are visiting.

Blocks

Blocks are another tool necessary if children are to learn to represent their world using symbols. Children can use a set of wooden unit blocks to build maps and re-create their world.

If wooden blocks are too expensive, you can make blocks from gallon, half-gallon, quart, and pint-sized empty paper milk or juice cartons or from shoe boxes. Stuff them solidly with newspaper so they'll have some stability and weight. If you have time, you can cover them with some type of durable paper.

Children's Books

Aberg, R., & Clidas, J. (2003). *Map keys (Rookie read-about geography series)*. New York: Children's Press.

Chesanow, N., & Jose, A. W. (1995). *Where do I live?* New York: Barron's Educational Series.

Cohen, C. L. (1996). *Where's the fly?* New York: Greenwillow.

Fanelli, S. (1995). *The map book*. New York: HarperCollins.

Hennessy, B. G. (2004). *The once upon a time map book*. New York: Candlewick Press.

Leedy, L. (2003). *Mapping Penny's world*. New York: Holt, Henry Books.

Murphy, S. J. (2004). *Treasure map*. New York: HarperCollins.

Rabe, T. (2002). *There's a map in my lap!* New York: Random House.

Other Resources

Board games such as "Candy Land," "Chutes and Ladders," and "Cherry Tree," which may be available from some lending libraries, introduce children to following paths like the ones they see on a map.

Map puzzles also give children practice with the idea that maps represent their world. You will also need

- paper, drawing tools, paste, scissors, and other art supplies

- brown and blue paper strips for building maps in the block area

- small wooden or plastic people and vehicles

The Home-School Connection

Children need many experiences using maps in order to gain an understanding of their use, scale, perspective, and symbols. During the year, as you continuously introduce children to maps and their use, ask parents to involve their children with mapping.

You might use one of the letters to parents on the tear out sheets on pages 116–117 at the end of this chapter. The letters could also be used as models for a newsletter.

◇ Evaluating and Assessing Children's Learning

Assessing children's map skills will be a continuous activity done on an individual and group basis using observations and structured interviews with individual children. You may want to use the evaluation tear out sheets on pages 119 and 120.

————————————— **FOR THE CHILDREN** —————————————

◇ Standard 1. Maps Use Lines, Color, and Other Symbols to Represent Reality and Are Used to Locate Oneself in Space

Children will need many experiences playing with and using maps to develop the idea that maps are symbols that stand for or represent the children's world.

◆ Plan walking field trips, perhaps inside the school, around the school building, or around the block. Take a walk in the school building or around the block. Before you start your walk, draw a large map of the route you will take. Use color and lines to symbolize the hallways or roads and streets you will follow and the things you and the children will observe along the way.

   As you walk, consult the map, showing children where their room or school is on the map and the route they will take. Point to things they see along the way and relate these to the symbols used on the map. When you return to the classroom, hang the map on the wall so you and the children can refer to it.

◆ Take a walking field trip at least once a week. Repeating the same trip permits children to consolidate their ideas and knowledge. Use a map for each of the trips.

◆ In the children's school, you might

   • visit the principal's or the director's office, the lunchroom, or the janitor's room to find out what jobs people in the school do

   • take another trip to the director's office to name all of the machines in the office that are used to communicate with others; you might find a telephone, fax machine, computer, or copying machine

   • walk through the school building to identify signs in the school that have words and that don't have words

   • visit another classroom

   • follow the water or heating pipes from your room to their source

   • use a map when preparing for a fire drill

◆ In the neighborhood, you might take a trip to

   • watch construction workers

   • identify the three most common plants in the neighborhood

   • visit behind the counter at a fast-food restaurant, post office, gas station, or other business

   • look at a neighbor's flowers

   • identify the materials used to build homes

   • find a bird's nest

   • have a picnic in the neighborhood park

   • name the different types of homes in the neighborhood

◆ Read S. Fanelli's *The Map Book* (1995) to 5-year-olds. Then make class books of maps. Children can draw maps of their own home, school, or neighborhood, or pretend maps of places they've never seen or places they would like to see, such as castles in Disneyland, a fantasy island, or their own Candy Land.

◆ When children arrive in your school or move away, consult maps and a globe to locate where they came from or will be moving to. The only goal is to familiarize children with the use of a globe or map, not to ask them to use cardinal directions or to locate places on the map.

◆   To involve children in sociodramatic play, create a floor map. A floor map is a rough map made to foster better play and thinking. After a trip through the community, use a big sheet of construction paper (perhaps joining several pieces) to make a map large enough to cover a section of the floor. On the map, draw the route taken on the trip. Draw symbols to suggest the buildings you saw, and tell the children what these were. Ask them to continue to build the map using blocks, drawing materials, play people, and vehicles.

◇   **Standard 2. Scale**

Scale is the concept that a map is a small picture of a much larger place.

◆   Introduce children to the idea of scale by looking at videos and photos of themselves and their families. Point out how small the children look, and tell them that maps are like the photographs. Maps represent their world, but like in the photographs, things seem much smaller than they actually are.

◆   Blocks permit children to re-create and express their perceptions, feelings, and ideas about the walking trips they've experienced. Hang one of the maps you've used on a trip near the block area. Add long strips of brown paper to the block area. Children can use these to re-create roads or streets. Blue paper can be used to represent lakes, rivers, or other bodies of water.

   After children have experienced building with blocks, you can add wooden or plastic people, houses, signs, and wheeled toys to the area that will enhance their building and play.

◆   Using blocks, you and the children can work together to make a map of their room or playground. After you have built the play yard or room using blocks, transfer this

Blocks allow a child to re-create and express her feelings, perceptions, and ideas about walking trips in the community.

work to paper. Using cut-out paper to represent furniture or play yard equipment, make a more permanent map of the room or yard.

◇ **Standard 3. Perspective**

Perspective is the concept that a map is a picture of a place as if you were looking at it from above, like a bird in the sky.

◆ Read C. L. Cohen's, book *Where's the Fly?* (1996), a book about how a fly sees the world while looking down from on high.

JUST PRETEND

Sometimes it is fun to pretend and use your imagination. You might ask children to "just pretend" and draw, paint, or construct a map using the following ideas:

- After you read M. Sendak's *Where the Wild Things Are* (1988), ask children to draw a map so others could find where the wild things live. What path would they take to find the wild things? How would they travel? What things might they see along the way?

- Read E. Field's poem, "Wynken, Blynken, and Nod," who one night sailed off in a wooden shoe on a river of crystal light into a sea of dew. Have children draw a map of the route through the sea of dew that Wynken, Blynken, and Nod traveled that night. What stars did they see? What else did they see?

- Read Robert McCloskey's *Blueberries for Sal* (1948). Then ask the children to make a map of the path Little Sal and her mother followed from their home to pick blueberries on the hill. Next they can draw the path the mother bear and her cub followed.

- Peter Rabbit made repeated visits to Mr. McGregor's garden. After you read several of Beatrix Potter's Peter Rabbit books, ask children to draw a map of the paths Peter Rabbit and his friends used to find their way into and out of the garden.

- D. Freeman wrote *Corduroy* (1968). What store was Corduroy lost in? Draw a map of the store.

- Where did Leo Lionni's *Swimmy* (1969) swim? Draw a map of Swimmy's world.

- How did Eric Carle's hungry caterpillar find lunch? Draw a map of the path the hungry caterpillar took.

Books to accompany "Just Pretend":
Carle, E. (1984). *The Hungry Caterpillar.* New York: Pantheon Books.
Field, E. (1904). *Poems of Childhood.* New York: Scribner & Sons.
Freeman, D. (1968). *Corduroy.* New York: Scholastic.
Lionni, L. (1969). *Swimmy.* New York: Pantheon Books.
McCloskey, R. (1948). *Blueberries for Sal.* New York: Viking.
Potter, B. (1903). *The Tale of Peter Rabbit.* London: Warne.
Sendak, M. (1988). *Where the Wild Things Are.* New York: HarperCollins Children's Books.

◆ Take the children to the top floor of the building or the top of a hill. Ask children to look at the world below them just as a bird flying high in the sky would look down. Talk about how small the world looks. Perhaps they can locate a popular fast-food restaurant, a parking lot, or some other place familiar to them. Then refer to a map, pointing out that it is like a picture of a place taken from above.

◇ **Reflecting**

Ask children to apply their knowledge of maps. Use the map of the room or yard you and the children made or create a new map to play hidden treasure. Hide an object, the treasure, someplace in the room or yard. Mark on the map the place the treasure is hidden. Have the children use the map to find the object. Do this first as a total group. Then make several maps so dyads, or small groups of children, can practice using the map to locate hidden treasure. After children have found the treasure, ask them as a group to describe how they knew where to look by using the map.

◇ **Extending and Expanding to the Early Primary Grades**

Primary-age children can do the following activities:

◆ See the world as if they were a fly. Take markers and paper out-of-doors, and have the children, in small groups or individually, climb to the top of a jungle gym or other piece of play yard equipment. Place objects under the gym, and ask children to describe these. How do the objects look when the children are above them? Can they tell what each one is? How? Then ask them to climb down and draw each object the way it looked when they were on top of the jungle gym. You might begin with a shoe, hat, book, or favorite toy. One teacher chose a small umbrella the children used during a walk in the rain. She opened it under the jungle gym and propped it up so the children looked down on an object that appeared to be round and flat.

◆ After they have drawn objects the way they look from above, the children can draw the same objects by looking directly at them. Compare the two drawings.

◆ Apply their knowledge of mapping by drawing, from memory, a map of their local community. Ask them to show the route they take to school, from their home to the local supermarket or shopping mall, and to and from parks and other recreational facilities.

◆ Read *Treasure Map* (Murphy, 2004). Place children in groups. Give each a secret treasure, perhaps a new book or game for the group. Have groups plan where to hide the treasure and then draw a map to the treasure. Groups exchange maps and go on a treasure hunt.

◆ *Map Keys* (Aberg & Clidas, 2003) can be used by primary children as they draw and interpret maps.

◇ **Documenting Children's Learning**

A web can document the learning, skills, and attitudes children gained playing with, using, and creating maps. The web might look like this, depending on the activities you implemented.

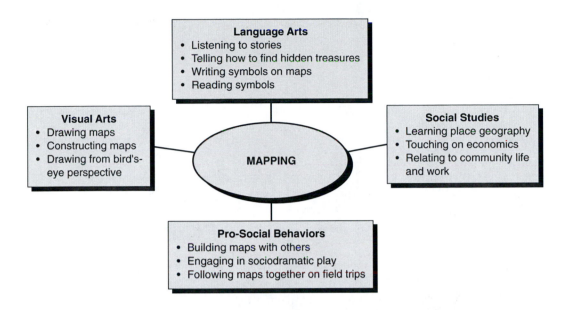

Hang the web in the hall, adding an explanation such as the following: "This year we have used maps. These are some of the things we learned."

◆ Mount some photographs you have taken of the children using maps on their walks around the school or playing or building with maps. Make a smaller copy of the web and explanation to send home to parents.

◆ Document individual children's mapmaking skills by placing their maps completed at the beginning of the year, the middle of the year, and the end of the school year in their portfolios.

◆ Make a class book. Ask children to draw a pretend map, or ask them to draw a map of their school, play yard, route to their home, or their room at home. Duplicate these for a class book so each child can have one to take home.

Date _____

Dear Parents:

This year we will be using maps inside and outside the classroom. We will draw and follow maps when we take walking field trips and will have small maps for children to play with as they pretend to take trips. The purpose of using maps is to help children learn that maps stand for a place, and that they help us locate ourselves in space.

You can help your children learn that maps stand for a place by using maps with them. When you take a trip, show them the route you will follow on a map. Point out the symbols that stand for the things you will see as you travel.

You might point to a school bell on the map that stands for their school, the markings that represent streets or railroad tracks, or the blue that represents a river or lake.

Thank you for helping us familiarize children with maps and how to use them.

Sincerely,

Date _____

Dear Parents:

We are using maps to locate hidden treasures in the play yard and in our room. This will help children learn that maps help people locate things in their world. You can help children become familiar with maps. The next time you are shopping at the mall, stop and look at a map of the place. Show your children the symbol that stands for where they are as you are looking at the map. Use your finger to point out the path you will follow to a store. Continue to consult the map as you shop and walk through the mall.

Sincerely,

Date _____

Dear Parents:

We wanted you to know that _____, a member of our class, is moving to _____ this week. One of the ways we are going to say good-bye is by writing _____'s new address on a chart in our room. We will then locate the new place on a map and talk about the things that will be there.

You might want to locate _____ on a map with your children. While you do so, you can show them where you were born, where you lived as a child, where other relatives live, or where you once thought you would like to live.

As you talk with your children about these different places, use the names of the cities, states, and nations. Show children the symbols that stand for rivers, mountains, or lakes. Talk about how people travel today, as well as how people traveled across our land in the past.

Sincerely,

Group Evaluation
Evaluating and Assessing Children's
Map Skills

How often and where do children play with maps?

Where?	How Often?	(Record Dates)
• housekeeping area		
• block area		
• with wheeled toys		
• other		

How often do children	Record Dates
• refer to maps as if they were taking a trip?	
• talk about something on a map?	
• consult a map as they are building/painting?	
• try to locate a place?	
• refer to scale (i.e., "This is much smaller")?	
• talk about perspective (i.e., "It's like a bird looking down")?	
• draw, paint, or build maps?	

Which children use maps?   **List Names**

Which children do not use maps?   **List Names**

Individual Evaluation
Evaluating and Assessing Children's
Map Skills

Name _____ Date _____

You will need a small map to show the child, plus paper and markers or crayons.

Show the child the map and ask

• What is this?

• What do we use it for?

• Why is the map so small?

Point to various symbols and ask

• What do these lines (street, highway) mean?

• What does this blue (river, lake, ocean) mean?

• What does this bell (school) mean?

Analyze children's responses. Judge each for

• accuracy

• completeness

• elaboration

Give the child a piece of paper and markers and ask her/him to draw a map of how she/he would go home from the school. Judge the map.

The child's map demonstrated

	Yes	No
• understanding of scale	_____	_____
• perspective	_____	_____
• use of symbols	_____	_____
• knowledge of place	_____	_____

9

Making and Keeping Friends

FOR THE TEACHER

◇ **What You'll Need to Know**

How does a child make and keep a friend? For very young children, it seems enough to be in the presence of one or two others. For them, a friend is defined as someone the child sees regularly in the neighborhood or the childcare center that will help build with blocks or play house.

As children grow and develop, however, it is extremely important for them to learn how to interact successfully with peers. Children who have friends

- seem to adjust more easily to school

- have fewer mental health problems

- have fewer adjustment difficulties in later years

The prevalence of violent solutions to conflicts, even between young children, suggests the need to concentrate on experiences that build a positive sense of self and teach social skills. It also appears that children who employ immature communication skills fail to form friendships with ease. So it is important that children learn the "right words" to use with others.

Popular children interact with others in appropriate ways, such as calling them by name and suggesting joint activities that would be of interest to all parties. They also appear to possess a sense of how to approach a group that is already playing by making a smooth and nondisruptive entry. While children mature at different rates in their ability to form and maintain friendships, teachers need to guide them in developing the skills that provide the basis for satisfying relationships. It is important that the teacher be sensitive and responsive to the need of neglected, developmentally delayed, aggressive, and culturally different children to find a place in the classroom community and to win the acceptance of peers.

◇ **Key Concepts Based on CTB and Curriculum Standards for Social Studies**

- The development of a firm sense of identity and self-efficacy is prerequisite to making and keeping friends (Domain 1, Self-knowledge, Social Skills, and Motivation to Learn, Guideline I, Children Will Develop Knowledge of Self, Guideline I, Goal 1, Objective 1, Children Will Develop Healthy Self-Concepts, Guideline I, Goal 1, Objective 2, Children Will Develop Healthy Self-Esteem, Guideline I, Goal 1, Objective 3, Children Will View Themselves as Efficacious, Capable Individuals Who Can Set Goals and Achieve Them, Guideline II, Goal 1, Objective 1, Children Will Develop Awareness of Others, Guideline II, Goal 1, Objective 2, Children Will Develop the Social Skills of Sharing and Cooperating

Note to the Teacher: It is necessary to keep in mind that in some of your settings, you will have children in your classroom who are homeless, who live with foster parents, or who live under such harsh conditions that the ideas presented here may not immediately work effectively with them. They may try your patience because their needs are so great. Helping these children to have a friend may be the most important thing you can do for them, yet you will have to exercise extra sensitivity and care in the process. You may well be their first friend.

with Others, CTB; Theme IV, Individual Development and Identity, Individuals, Groups, and Institutions, Curriculum Standards for Social Studies).

- To interact effectively with others, children must learn to express feelings and take the perspectives of others (Domain 1, Self-Knowledge, Social Skills, and Motivation to Learn, Guideline II, Children Will Develop Knowledge of Others and Social Skills, CTB Standards Theme IV, Individual Development and Identity, Curriculum Standards for Social Studies).

- Children can be assisted in utilizing effective strategies for making and keeping friends (Domain 1, Guideline II, CTB, see previous text; Theme IV, Curriculum Standards for Social Studies, see previous text).

- Children can be assisted in finding and using effective strategies for resolving conflicts (see previous text).

◇ Goals and Objectives

Children will develop a firm sense of identity through positive interactions with parents, teachers, and peers.

Children will learn to express their feelings about relationships and will learn that their peers hold similar feelings.

Through coaching, modeling, and role-playing, children will learn effective strategies for making and keeping friends.

Through coaching, modeling, the use of logical consequences, and role-playing, children will learn to resolve conflicts effectively.

◇ What You'll Need

Children's Books

There are many children's books that deal with

- peer relationships
- children's fears of not having friends
- the problems of making friends in new situations, such as moving from another city or country
- the emotions that surround conflict situations with friends
- entering school or making the transition to a new school
- expressing feelings

Some of the best books are

Aliki. (1982). *We are best friends*. New York: Greenwillow.

Bang, M. (1999). *When sophie gets angry—Really, really angry*. New York: The Blue Sky Press.

Cohen, M. (1967). *Will I have a friend?* New York: Macmillan Publishing Co.

Cohen, M. (1971). *Best friends*. New York: Macmillan Publishing Co.

Hallinan, P. K. (2002). *A rainbow of friends.* Ideals Publications.

Havill, J. (1996). *Jamaica and Brianna.* New York: Houghton Mifflin.

Johnson, A. (1992). *The leaving morning.* New York: Orchard Books.

Keats, E. J. (1978). *The trip.* New York: Greenwillow Books.

Kellogg, S. (1986). *Best friends.* New York: Dial Books for Young Readers.

Rohmann, E. (2002). *My friend rabbit.* Brookfield, CT: Roaring Brook Press.

Ross, D. (1999). *A book of friends.* New York: HarperCollins Publishers.

Udry, J. M. (1961). *Let's be enemies.* New York: Harper & Row Publishers.

Zolotow, C. (1969). *The hating book.* New York: Harper & Row Publishers.

Other Things You'll Need

You may want to reinforce your belief in the importance of social/emotional skills. An excellent new book is D. Gartrell's *The Power of Guidance: Teaching Social-Emotional Skills in Early Childhood Classrooms.* (2004, published by NAEYC).

Another excellent resource for grades 2 to 5 is the *Don't Laugh at Me* curriculum by Peter Yarrow, which is distributed by his organization, Operation Respect (*www.dontlaugh.org*). Other excellent resources include:

- Learning centers where children may find common interests and act out common problems

- A felt board and characters to illustrate friendships and conflict situations; you may want to store the characters in a marked envelope so children can create their own stories

- A writing center equipped with materials for letter and postcard writing

- Little boxes in which children can receive notes sent from classmates

It's fun to share a common interest.

- Art materials

- Old magazines

- Mirrors

- Pictures of the children in your class and their families

- Posters of diverse children and their families

- Puppets

- A simple stage

- Tapes of music with different emotional content

The Home-School Connection

Parents are usually very concerned about whether their children are making or have friends. Mrs. Bowman went into the observation room of the university childcare center to see if Bettina was playing with other children. She was pleased to see that her daughter was busy at the water table with several other boys and girls.

Often parents who are not native English speakers fear that their children will be isolated because of language differences. Parents whose children are differently abled are very worried that teachers and classmates will find them difficult and fail to meet their needs for positive attention and friendship. Through frequent communications and newsletters, you can reassure parents that your curriculum emphasizes making and keeping friends for everyone.

You may want to use the tear out sheet on page 132 at the end of this chapter or modify it to meet your needs.

◇ Evaluating and Assessing Children's Learning

Children's progress at making and keeping friends will be assessed throughout the year using

- observations

- small- and large-group discussions

- portfolios of children's work

- children's self-evaluations

The tear out sheet on page 133 can be used at different points in the school year to chart growth in children's self-concepts, expressions of feelings, perspective taking, and ability to resolve conflicts.

——————————— FOR THE CHILDREN ———————————

◇ Standard 1. Forming a Positive Sense of Self

With assistance, children are capable of forming a positive sense of self-esteem and self-efficacy. The CTB Standards point out that the two differ. Self-esteem refers to judgments children make about their worth or how they value themselves. Self-efficacy is the belief that one can achieve a task by using one's own capabilities (CTB, 2003).

◆   On the first day of school, read M. Cohen's *Will I Have a Friend?* (1967). Ask children how many of them are afraid that they will not find new friends to play with. Ask them to pick an activity center and tell them that like the characters in the book, they will find friends as they work with materials and play with toys.

◆   Names are an important part of a person's identity. Post children's names at child level with their pictures below the names. Encourage children to find out the origins of their names and explain them to the class.

◆   Sing name songs so children will quickly learn each other's names. Substitute children's names in stories, poems, and games.

◆   Use children's names whenever possible. Help them make name cards. Mix the cards up and have the children find their own names or the name of a friend.

◆   Have the children create a newsletter for themselves and their families. Have them include news stories about children in the class. Make sure each child is included.

◆   Place mirrors in the creative dramatic area for children to use, and give children feedback as they look at themselves: "How pretty your blue eyes are, Cynthia. Does anyone else in your family have blue eyes?" "You seem to be growing taller every day." Have children dictate a story to you describing their appearances.

◆   Have children draw or paint pictures and dictate stories to you about the things that they can do. Compile a class book of the things that children in your classroom can do. Share it with the children, and put it in the reading center for children to use alone or in groups. Emphasize that these children can do so many things.

◆   Through newsletters and personal communications with parents, emphasize the need to build a strong sense of identity and self-efficacy in children. Suggest ways that children can be recognized at home for the many things they can do.

Children express their positive feelings about each other in many ways.

◆ Make sure that children understand that they can have many different kinds of friends. Put up signs and posters in the languages of children in your class. Sing and listen to songs in different languages. Teach children simple words, such as the parts of the body, in diverse languages.

◆ Read Eric Rohmann's *My Friend Rabbit* (2002). Ask the children if they have friends who don't always do everything right or friends that have hurt them accidentally. Record the children's responses. Emphasize that friends try hard but that they are not always perfect. Discuss how we need to support friends when they fail to do things right.

◇ Standard 2. Recognizing Their Feelings and the Feelings of Others

◆ Read C. Zolotow's *The Hating Book* (1969). Have children describe how they feel when a friend suddenly becomes an enemy. Have children discuss whether they would feel the same way as the character in the book. Then ask them what they could do to get their friend back. Make a T-chart. Use two columns on poster board entitled "Feelings" and "Things I Could Do." Discuss the strategies for resuming the friendship and decide with the children whether or not they would work.

Feelings	Things I Could Do
lonely	invite him to my house

◆ At group time, use two puppets to pose a problem: "This puppet has spilled paint on the other puppet's picture. How do you think the other puppet feels?" "This puppet won't let the other puppet play with the trucks. How do you think the other puppet feels?"

◆ Communicate to the children your understanding of what they are feeling and the reasons for it. "You feel very angry now because Carl knocked you down on his way to the bike." "You're happy because the children made you the leader."

◆ Read E. J. Keats' *The Trip* (1978). Ask children how they would feel if they moved to a new neighborhood where they didn't know anybody, not even the dogs and the cats. Have them dictate a sentence about their feelings. Put the sentences together to make a visual display. Have the children make pictures to add to the display. Then have them listen to tapes of different types of music, and discuss with the class which music best depicts their feelings.

◆ Read Aliki's *We Are Best Friends* (1982). Ask children how they would feel if their best friend moved away. Have them dictate a sentence about their feelings. Since the character in the book, Robert, resolved his problem by drawing a picture-letter to his friend, have the children write picture-letters to imaginary or real friends who have moved away.

◇ **Standard 3. Learning How to Make and Keep Friends**

Most children are capable of learning how to make and keep friends.

◆   Have children create personal mailboxes for the writing center. Encourage them to make cards for their classmates. Help children to dictate a sentence, and write it and the name of the child on the card. Keep a record to make sure that everyone is receiving messages. If not, have children pick a name from a hat and write a personal card or postcard. Cards or letters may be illustrated.

◆   Read J. M. Udry's *Let's Be Enemies* (1961). Ask children if they have ever been angry with a friend. Have them list the reasons why. Encourage them to think of all the good things they did with their friend. Have the children draw two children as enemies, then draw two children as friends.

◆   In helping children who are having difficulty making friends, the following may be useful:

  • When organizing children for play, group children lacking in social skills with those who are more competent.

  • Pair a developmentally disabled child with a younger peer.

  • Provide direct teaching. For example, tell the group in the housekeeping center that Angelina can be the mother. Or ask Helen to tell the girls what she wants instead of crying.

◆   Make sure that activities are structured so that everyone can be successful and receive recognition.

◇ **Standard 4. Resolving Conflicts Effectively**

Most children are capable of resolving conflicts effectively.

◆   Try to anticipate situations that will cause conflicts. For example, many fights occur during transitions from one activity to another or when children have to wait for long periods of time. Minimize waiting times, and be prepared with songs and finger plays to keep children busy while others are getting ready. Also try the following:

  • Select or develop games that avoid or minimize competition.

  • Use group art projects such as murals to which everyone contributes. Point out how much more can be accomplished when children share the responsibility.

  • Model caring and cooperation with the children. Share your ideas in a cooperative way. Demonstrate respect for their ideas and decisions.

◆   Teach children to use words rather than aggressive actions to gain their goal or to stop a conflict. Teach them to speak directly to each other rather than through the teacher.

◆   Involve children in discussion or role-playing about alternative solutions to problems and their consequences at times when conflicts are not occurring. Use the felt board to simulate a conflict situation and list the solutions that children reach.

◆ Make sure that the consequences of aggressive acts are directly related to the misbehaviors. These include doing something kind for the victim or practicing alternative behaviors immediately.

◆ There are times when children *do* need to share resources in the classroom, such as when there are simply not enough blocks or puzzles to go around. They also need to share the teacher's attention. Make it clear to children under what circumstances it is necessary to share and when they can say no. Discuss with children the benefits of sharing and have them write a group story, "Why We Share."

◆ Coach children who are anxious to enter a group but don't know how. Teach them to use the "right words" rather than disrupt the game. They may need to learn to wait for a period until an appropriate time.

◆ Teach social techniques to class members who interact with differently abled children. Recognize and reinforce efforts to interact. Teach patience and caring.

◇ Reflecting and Reaching Conclusions

Have children *apply* their knowledge of making and keeping friends.

◆ Use the class project—the *Friendship Book*—composed of entries from children and parents. Make a list of the qualities that children value in good friends. Make another list of parents' views of friendship. Compare the lists. How are they the same? How are they different? Make a Venn Diagram to display the information in graphic form.

◆ Have children make individual *Friendship Books* and share them with the class. Friends may be classmates, friends from home, or imaginary friends. Emphasize that children can have many different kinds of friends and friends of different ages.

◆ Either the teacher or a group of children can create a puppet show or play illustrating a conflict situation. The other children can then dramatize a solution or solutions.

◆ Keep a list of words that help children make and keep friends on a chart or in a box. When children are having a problem, suggest that they consult the words and find the right ones for their situation.

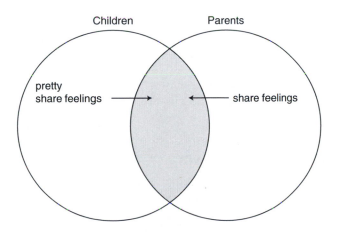

◇ Extending and Expanding to the Early Primary Grades

In general, primary-age children are quite concerned about friendships. They expect their friends to share feelings with them, be available when they need them, and not reveal confidences. Yet, they often need help in evaluating the quality of their friendships. Parents and caregivers also have concerns about children's friends.

Early primary-age children can do the following:

◆ Evaluate situations in the books they read. Read R. and L. Hoban's *Best Friends for Frances,* which provides multiple examples of conflicts between friends. Ask the children who did the right thing: "How did they all become friends again?"

◆ Evaluate the quality of a friendship. Ask children to provide reasons why someone is a good friend. List the reasons. Then have children decide what they would do if they believed that a friendship was harmful to them. For example, what would they do if they believed their friend would get them into trouble?

◆ Concepts of community service can begin in the early primary grades. Extend their knowledge of making and keeping friends to caring for those in the classroom or community that have special needs. Children might make a decision to donate food, clothing, or art materials to a childcare center for homeless children. If possible, they should visit the center or have the center send them pictures of the children.

◆ Profit from the opinions of important models in their lives. Have teachers and aides bring in pictures of their best friends and have them discuss why they chose that person.

◆ Make appointments with school personnel and interview them about the qualities of their best friends. Questions should be prepared in advance and responses reported to the class. Children can organize the data by the number of people that chose a particular quality in a friend. With the help of the teacher, the data could be represented in bar graph form.

◆ Research and learn about historical figures who are of interest to them. Children may use reference books to identify great friends of the past.

◆ Widen their worlds and express their thoughts and feelings in writing. Teachers can arrange a cooperative venture with a classroom somewhere else in the country. Children can exchange pictures, projects, and newsletters. For interested children, pen pals may be arranged with the careful supervision of the teacher.

◆ Utilize computers to communicate with children around the world. Teachers must make sure that children find suitable international friends.

◇ Documenting Children's Learning

A web can document the learning, skills, attitudes, and behaviors children gained through their unit, "Making and Keeping Friends." Hang the web in a spot where it can be seen by visitors and children. Children may add to the web as the year progresses and they learn more about friendships. Ask the children to provide titles for the web such as "We Are Learning to Make and Keep All Kinds of Friends."

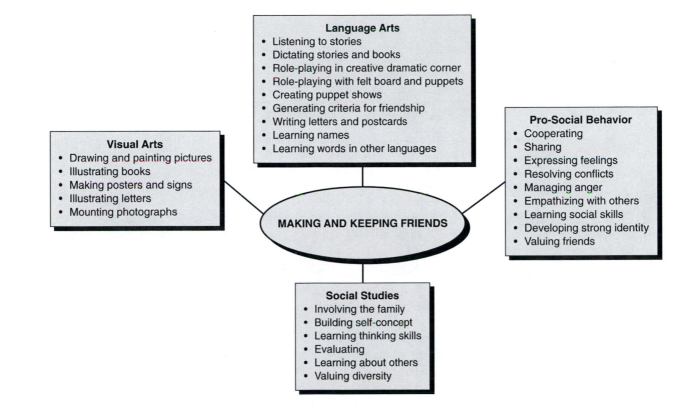

Language Arts
- Listening to stories
- Dictating stories and books
- Role-playing in creative dramatic corner
- Role-playing with felt board and puppets
- Creating puppet shows
- Generating criteria for friendship
- Writing letters and postcards
- Learning names
- Learning words in other languages

Pro-Social Behavior
- Cooperating
- Sharing
- Expressing feelings
- Resolving conflicts
- Managing anger
- Empathizing with others
- Learning social skills
- Developing strong identity
- Valuing friends

Visual Arts
- Drawing and painting pictures
- Illustrating books
- Making posters and signs
- Illustrating letters
- Mounting photographs

MAKING AND KEEPING FRIENDS

Social Studies
- Involving the family
- Building self-concept
- Learning thinking skills
- Evaluating
- Learning about others
- Valuing diversity

Date _____

Dear Parents:

As part of our curriculum this year, we are working on the theme of making and keeping friends. Your children will be learning to express their feelings in positive ways, show sympathy and kindness for other children, cooperate in classroom activities, share with others, and solve conflicts in nonaggressive or nonviolent ways. Since you are their most important teachers, we hope that you will model these behaviors and encourage them in your children. To be good friends, children also need to know that they are valued. Perhaps you could praise your children for the many positive, interesting, and creative things that we know they do at home.

As an important part of our emphasis on making and keeping friends, we are making a Friendship Book. Children will dictate and illustrate their stories about friends, but the most important part will come from families. We would like you to contribute to our book by telling us about your friends and friendships through the years. Please send in pictures, drawings, letters, invitations, or any remembrances of friends, and a short article about your friendships. Tell us why these persons were good friends.

If you are a nonnative speaker, don't worry! We will have your article translated. The teachers and your children are excited about the Friendship Book. Anything that you contribute will be greatly appreciated. And remember, if you would like to make some new friends, come to our Parent Room, have some coffee, and talk with other parents. Bring your other children; there are plenty of toys and books to keep them busy.

We are looking forward to hearing from you about your friends.

Sincerely,

Date _____

Name _____

Age of Child _____

Individual Evaluation: Assessing Children's Skills at Making and Keeping Friends

	Always	Sometimes	Never
Exhibits pride in work and play activities.	_____	_____	_____
Initiates activities.	_____	_____	_____
Expresses feelings appropriately.	_____	_____	_____
Exhibits self-control.	_____	_____	_____
Shows concern and empathy for others, including those with special needs.	_____	_____	_____
Communicates well with others, using appropriate words.	_____	_____	_____
Expresses wants and needs verbally.	_____	_____	_____
Shows appropriate physical contact.	_____	_____	_____
Shares toys, activities, and attention.	_____	_____	_____
Enters a new group appropriately.	_____	_____	_____
Responds to ideas and requests from the teacher and other children.	_____	_____	_____
Deals with aggression.	_____	_____	_____
Plays cooperatively.	_____	_____	_____
Exhibits an appropriate level of assertiveness.	_____	_____	_____
Models appropriate behavior for others.	_____	_____	_____
Attempts to resolve conflicts appropriately by using words and avoiding aggression.	_____	_____	_____
Chooses different types of friends for various activities.	_____	_____	_____

10

Wants and Needs
Beginning Economic Concepts

─────── **FOR THE TEACHER** ───────

◇ **What You'll Need to Know**

Ms. Kitchen, teacher of the 4-year-olds' group, said in dismay to her colleagues, "These children have and want so much that I am really concerned about them." She discussed accepting the responsibility to make them more informed and better consumers. While children are not ready to reason abstractly about economic issues until they reach the age of 10 or 11, they encounter economic concepts daily and express a high level of interest in them. Since adult illiteracy about economics is widespread in our society, you may want to introduce economics to children early so they will be ready to make wise personal economic decisions as consumers, workers, and citizens. Economics also plays an important part in local, national, and international public policy, so an understanding of economic concepts will eventually enable children to live in an increasingly interdependent world.

As with all areas of the social studies, children build their knowledge of economics from simple and concrete to more complex through active experiences. Three-year-olds can distinguish between money and other objects, but they don't know what is worth more or less. Some 3-year-olds are not aware that money is needed to purchase things from the store, yet they do pretend to pay for things. They also know the difference between "yours" and "mine," and can identify some adult activities as "work."

Older preschool children understand that it is necessary to have money to purchase things, but they still believe that the larger the coin, the more it is worth. To them, one works and gets money, rather than one gets money because one works. Kindergarten and young elementary children know that you need enough money to pay for a purchase, can distinguish between the various denominations of coins, and know which will buy more things. They also have some idea of paid occupations and can name those with which they have had experience such as the person who delivers their mail.

Strand VII of the *Curriculum Standards for Social Studies* (NCSS, 1994) concerns production, distribution, and consumption. According to the authors, while young children are not ready to apply advanced economic reasoning, "young learners begin by differentiating between wants and needs" (p. 27).

◇ **Key Concepts Based on Curriculum Standards for Social Studies**

- Scarcity means that there is always a conflict between never-ending wants and limited resources.

- Since resources are limited, people must choose some things and give up others.

- People produce and consume. When they produce, they make goods. When they consume, they use goods and services.

- Money and trading or bartering are used to obtain goods and services.

- People work in a variety of jobs.

- Helping others who do not have their basic needs met is socially desirable.

◇ **Goals and Objectives**

Children will identify choices they have made and explain why they had to make a choice.

Children will identify persons who produce goods.

Children will identify persons using goods and services and describe the goods and services being consumed.

Children will identify exchanges they have made and tell whether they were monetary or barter exchanges.

Children will identify persons doing various types of jobs and begin to understand the duties and responsibilities involved in work.

Children will identify projects designed to help others to meet their basic needs.

◇ What You'll Need

Through active experiences, both planned and incidental, basic economic concepts will be emphasized over the early childhood years and integrated into all areas of the curriculum.

Reference Books

The following three books will give you some ideas for children's experiences:

Berg, A., & Berg Bochner, A. (1993). *The totally awesome money book for kids and their parents.* New York: Newmarket Press.
Godfrey, N. S. (1998). *Ultimate kids' money book.* New York: Simon and Schuster.
Nathan, A., & Palen, D. (1998). *The kids' allowance book.* New York: Walker and Co.

Children's Books

There are a number of children's books under the category of mathematics/money/scarcity. Some of the better ones for young children are:

Schwartz, D. (1985). *How much is a million?* New York: Lothrop, Lee, & Shepard.
Schwartz, D. (1989). *If you made a million.* New York: Lothrop, Lee, & Shepard.
Viorst, J. (1978). *Alexander, who used to be rich last Sunday.* New York: Atheneum.
Wells, R. (1997). *Bunny money.* New York: Dial Books for Young Readers.
Williams, V. (1982). *A chair for my mother.* New York: Greenwillow.

You may want to look at books related to other important economic concepts. For example, in M. Brown's *Arthur's TV Trouble* (1995), Arthur learns the hard way that the products advertised on TV are not always as they seem.

Environmental issues are related to scarcity and choices. You might use D. Kuhn's *The Hidden Life of the Pond* (1988) to suggest ways children can help to save our environment. Two other beautiful books related to scarcity are:

Brother eagle, sister sky: A message from Chief Seattle. (1991). New York: Dial Books.
Czernecki, S., & Rhodes, T. (1994). *The humming birds' gift.* New York: Hyperion Books for Children.

Production and consumption are illustrated in:

MacHotka, H. (1992). *Pasta factory.* New York: Houghton Mifflin.
McMillan, B. (1996). *Jelly beans for sale.* New York: Scholastic.

Other Things You'll Need

- Centers of interest such as stores, offices, and factories that permit children to practice economic concepts.

- Nonstereotypical "dress up" clothing appropriate for various jobs. These may be recycled from children's homes.

- Props such as typewriters, stamps, ink pads, receipts, cash registers, play money, bins or boxes for holding goods, and empty food boxes.

- Recycled magazines with photographs of people at work and people consuming goods.

- Charts for recording children's wants and needs, job preferences, and comparisons between jobs.

- Folk songs with a job or work theme.

- Bins for classroom materials to be recycled or reused.

- Art materials.

- Large poster board for making signs.

Outdoor space may be utilized to emphasize environmental awareness. Children enjoy cleaning up a playground or adopting a stream.

The Home-School Connection

Parents are a valuable part of your economics curriculum. Children experience economics with their parents as they go to a variety of places where goods and services are offered, such as the supermarket, the laundry, a department store, or a restaurant. Through frequent communications such as a weekly newsletter or notice of a special event, you'll want to ask parents to discuss economic concepts with their children as they occur at home and in school.

For example, children observe the exchange of money for items that are needed or wanted by their families. Some parents take children to the bank to open their own accounts to save the money they have received for birthday or holiday gifts. Encourage parents to discuss choices with children. Which toys would the children like given that the family cannot afford them all? Which choices would they like to make for the future? Parents can also lead the way in prompting their children to reuse and recycle goods that the family consumes.

You may want to use one of the three tear out sheets on pages 145–147 at the end of this chapter or modify them to meet your needs.

◇ Evaluating and Assessing Children's Learning

Assessing children's economic concepts of scarcity, making choices, production and consumption, money and trade, and the interdependence of various jobs will be a continuous activity done on an individual and group basis using

- observations

- small- and large-group discussions

- parental feedback

- portfolios of children's work

- games

- children's self-evaluations and dictated stories about choices, persons who produce goods, persons who consume goods, buying and selling, and the content of various types of jobs

The tear out sheets on pages 148–149 at the end of this chapter can be used at different points in the school year to chart growth in children's knowledge of economic concepts, and to help you plan your curriculum.

FOR THE CHILDREN

◇ Standard 1. Identifying Wants, Needs, and Choices

Children are capable of identifying choices they have made because of the conflict between "needs" and "wants."

◆ Create a restaurant in the dramatic play area. Have children write and illustrate a menu with the cost of various items of food. Provide play money and have the children make choices based on how much money they have and how much the items cost.

◆ Create a store in the creative dramatic corner complete with bins to hold merchandise, a cash register, play money, stamps, pads for receipts, and props for the workers and consumers. One group of 4-year-olds decided to have a fruit market. They made signs in the various languages spoken by the children in the group with pictures to depict each fruit. They put these on the bins with the merchandise. Then they put a large sign with prices next to the pictures and words. The teacher gave

Children learn to make choices between their wants and needs.

each child enough money to purchase one item, so the children had to choose what they most wanted.

◆   Have the children choose one toy from a list of four, and dictate a sentence about what they gave up in making the choice.

◆   Have the children create a collage representing goods that they or their families consume now. Then, have them make another collage of things that they or their families would like to consume in the future.

◆   Take the kindergarten class to a restaurant. Mr. Amali's class decided on the House of Kabobs where they would learn a little more about their teacher's culture as well as sample the food of Pakistan. Mr. Amali gave the children a menu to study before the trip, and their parents gave them enough money for one dish. The children had to make effective decisions as consumers. When they got to the restaurant, Shana, Harry, and Juan decided that they would share their dishes so they could have more choices and taste more good food. Other children picked one type of kabob to eat.

◆   Read M. Brown's *Arthur's TV Trouble* (1995), and have the children dictate either an individual or group story about bad choices they have made.

◆   Have the children draw, paint, or write about a good choice they have made. In a small or large group, discuss why they were good choices.

◆   Pose problems for the children in large and small groups:

   • The school has only so much land. Some of the teachers and workers would like to use more of it for a parking lot since they drive to school. The principal and other workers would prefer to keep the garden and the trees. It is impossible to use the land for both purposes. What would the children choose? Why?

   • The director of the school has said that there is enough money for one new piece of playground equipment. What would they choose? Why?

◇   **Standard 2. Learning About Production and Consumption**

Children can identify and have active experiences with persons who produce and consume goods and services, and can describe the goods and services being produced and consumed.

◆   Have the children draw or paint pictures representing themselves or their family members as producers or workers. Have them dictate a story about what is being produced.

◆   Take several field trips around the school building. Assist the children in formulating questions for various persons who make the school run, such as the custodian, a secretary, the cook, and the principal.

◆   Visit a family member at work. Have the children prepare a list of questions to ask. It is best if the workplace provides hands-on experiences.

◆   Invite a family member to share his or her work with the class. Again, it is best if the family member can provide experiences for the children such as working with clay or weaving.

◆   Plan for the children to be producers. This activity may culminate in the Market Day suggested in the parent newsletter. Children may cook and may make stabiles, mobiles, dolls, and games using recycled materials. These can be sold to family members for small amounts of money. The money may be donated to a shelter for homeless children or another worthy cause chosen by the children.

◆ Have the children draw or paint pictures representing themselves or their family members as consumers.

◆ Ask children to think about the things they consume, and then to make a collage representing these things from recycled magazines.

◆ In small or large groups, children can make a shopping list and visit the local store to buy items that they will later consume.

◇ Standard 3. Identifying Monetary and Barter Exchanges

Children will identify exchanges they have made and tell whether they were monetary or barter exchanges.

◆ Ask children to recall times when they traded one thing to get something else that they wanted. As Natalia said, "I loved my nested dolls, but I wanted Troy's truck so bad that I traded my dolls." Chart the number of things that the children have traded and the types of trades.

◆ In addition to providing field experiences where money is exchanged, teach children to play games by counting and exchanging money. Younger children will play at making change. For a small group of older children, give each one 25 pennies, 5 nickels, 2 dimes, and a quarter in a cup. Provide them with dice. Children take turns rolling the dice and putting the amount of money required by the number on the dice in the middle of the table. They may trade pennies for nickels and so on. The child with the most money left is the winner. The game should be repeated often so there are many winners.

◆ Have children make change for their family members at Market Day.

Field experiences help a child to understand monetary exchanges.

◇ **Standard 4. Learning About Work**

Children will identify persons doing various types of jobs and begin to understand the duties and responsibilities involved in work. The following activities can be done in addition to the activities previously suggested for production and consumption and for exchanges:

◆ Have children interview their family members about the duties and responsibilities involved in their work. Produce a newsletter describing these.

◆ Children may further interview community members and make a list of duties involved in their work.

◆ Sing and dramatize work songs. Two good teacher resource books are:

   Blood, P., & Patterson, A. (Eds.). (1992). *Rise up singing: The group singing songbook.* Bethlehem, PA: Sing Out Corporation.
   Krull, K. (1992). *Gonna sing my head off! American folk songs for children.* New York: Alfred A. Knopf, Inc.

◆ Arrange the creative dramatic and block centers so that they reflect different types of work. Have children identify their duties when they were the doctor or the mommy.

◇ **Reflecting**

Have children apply their knowledge of economic concepts.

◆ Help them make better consumer choices. Make a chart of wants and needs for (a) children and (b) their families. Have children reflect on why needs come before wants. Make another chart of wants only. Have children make choices about the wiser purchase.

◆ Pose a problem: The children can have one additional purchase for the classroom. Should they choose the set of wooden blocks or the set of coloring books?

◆ Pose another problem about understanding jobs and their interdependence: First ask children to identify the duties of the bus driver (any school worker will do). Then ask them what would happen if the bus driver didn't report for work. Record the answers on chart paper.

◆ Post photographs from Market Day. Have children identify what they were doing in each photograph. Were they producers or consumers? Were they providing goods or services? Keep the photographs posted through the school year.

◆ On chart paper, record children's job preferences. Then have them compare the duties and responsibilities involved in each job.

◆ Read R. Wells' *Bunny Money* (1997). Ask the children to describe what life would be like if we all behaved like these bunnies. How did Ruby and Max learn the value of money? Have children chart the sequence of events that led to the happy ending.

◆ For practice, devise other simple games that involve making change with small denominations of money.

◇ **Extending and Expanding to the Early Primary Grades**

Primary children can do the following:

◆ Enjoy and participate in games. Have the children identify workers and paste pictures of them on cardboard cards. Create other cards with duties and responsibilities. Children will match the worker cards with the duties and responsibilities cards.

◆ Participate in some critical analysis. Have children watch a commercial at home or tape a commercial for them to view at school. Have them generate criteria for judging the commercial for honesty and accuracy in advertising. Then have a discussion about the merits of the commercial and the product that it is attempting to sell.

◆ Understand that others have needs that are more important than their own needs. Have children interview an elderly person or a person who is challenged in some way. They may write an informational column for the newsletter indicating why some people's needs may be greater than their needs. Discuss the importance of "helping" others whose most basic needs are not being met. As part of the Market Day celebration, have children raise money for the different social service agencies in their community that help those with basic needs. The children could then choose (or vote) on which agency will receive the proceeds from the fundraiser.

◆ Have a concern for the environment. Children may bring in clothing and other props to be recycled in the creative dramatic corner. Further, they may sort classroom articles into bins to be recycled. If possible, a field trip may be arranged to follow the recycling truck so that the children understand the entire process.

◆ Participate in refurbishing or enhancing the school environment. They may paint, clean, provide aesthetic enrichment, or plant a garden to enrich the school.

◆ Understand that people have different needs. You may enable them to have a pal in another city or state or even in another country. They may discuss their differing needs via e-mail or through letter writing.

◆ Keep a journal of the purchases they make, why they make them, and what they had to give up.

◆ For older elementary children, read *Brother Eagle, Sister Sky: A Message from Chief Seattle* (1991). Direct children to the last few pages of illustrations by Susan Jeffers. Ask them to dictate sentences about them. One column can be about Native Americans. The second column should relate to something that is destroying the environment near their homes or schools. Be ready with prompts since this is a difficult exercise, but very worthwhile.

◇ **Documenting Children's Learning**

A web can document the learning, skills, and attitudes generated through the emphasis on economic concepts. Hang the web in a place where it can be seen by visitors as well as the children. Add an explanation such as "This Year We Have Learned About Economics."

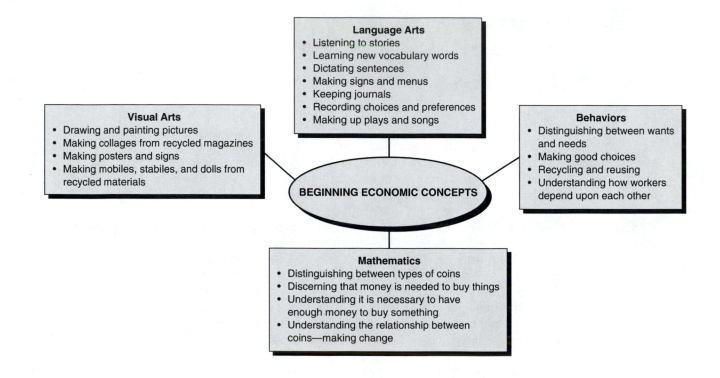

Language Arts
- Listening to stories
- Learning new vocabulary words
- Dictating sentences
- Making signs and menus
- Keeping journals
- Recording choices and preferences
- Making up plays and songs

Visual Arts
- Drawing and painting pictures
- Making collages from recycled magazines
- Making posters and signs
- Making mobiles, stabiles, and dolls from recycled materials

BEGINNING ECONOMIC CONCEPTS

Behaviors
- Distinguishing between wants and needs
- Making good choices
- Recycling and reusing
- Understanding how workers depend upon each other

Mathematics
- Distinguishing between types of coins
- Discerning that money is needed to buy things
- Understanding it is necessary to have enough money to buy something
- Understanding the relationship between coins—making change

Date _____

Dear Parents:

As part of our curriculum this year, we are helping your children to identify some important economic concepts. To do this, they need active, concrete experiences in thinking critically about several important issues that we have identified. We need your help!

First, children must distinguish between things that they want and things that they need. If your children are like most, they will want many things that they cannot have because of the lack of money to buy them. This is especially true because of the pressure of television advertising and things that their friends may have. We all have to learn that we can't have everything that we want because resources are scarce.

Here's how you can help. Discuss with your children the things that families need—the basic things are shelter, food, and clothing. Also talk to them about other things that you have been able to buy to make life more comfortable, such as a television set, and things that you would like to have for the future. Ask your children to tell you some of the things they want. Have them decide if they really need these things. Also, allow them to choose something they would really like to have that they have seen advertised. (This should not be a serious expense for you.) When the toy or game arrives, help them to decide if it was worth giving up something else to get the new item. Sometimes children learn best by making poor choices.

Thank you for your assistance with our economics project. We will be back with more ideas soon. Also stay tuned for news about our big, exciting Market Day, which will mark the end of our formal economics unit. Everyone will be invited. Come one and all.

Sincerely,

Date _____

Dear Parents:

How did your "wants" and "needs" discussions go? We have had some good feedback from some of you who even think it will help you with the demands of the holidays. We found that the children had a much better understanding of the concept of scarcity after they discussed it with you. We will be doing more things in class, such as having them identify the "wants" and "needs" for their classroom and playground.

Well, now we have another request! We have begun to explore the various jobs that people do and why these jobs are essential if things are going to work well at home, at school, and in the community. We would be delighted if some of you would come to school or invite us to your workplace to discuss your job and why people depend on you.

We would be honored if others of you would volunteer to spend a little time with us so that we may expand our knowledge of jobs people do. You may also want to discuss with your children how your home works because various family members do various jobs. What would it be like if these jobs were not done? No dinner? No clean clothes?

Again, thank you so much for your efforts to make our year a success.

Sincerely,

Market Day at School

On _____

At _____

Come one and all. Baby-sitting provided.

Date _____

Dear Parents:

Your children (with some help from their teachers and
aides) have created a Market Day for you, your families,
and friends. There will be art, charts, and stories
depicting various economic concepts. For your pleasure,
the children have been in the kitchen producing all types
of good food for you to buy, eat, and enjoy. There will
be a puppet show at _____ called "Jobs People Do." There
will be a small entrance fee. Nothing will cost more than
a dime. The children have learned to make change with
pennies, nickels, and dimes through playing games, and
will demonstrate their skill for you. See you there.

Sincerely,

Observation—Economic Terms

Date _____

Center/Area _____

Children's Names _____

Economic Terms Used (Record terms or words used)

	Accuracy		
	Not at All	Some	Accurate
1.	_____	_____	_____
2.	_____	_____	_____
3.	_____	_____	_____
4.	_____	_____	_____
5.	_____	_____	_____
6.	_____	_____	_____
7.	_____	_____	_____
8.	_____	_____	_____
9.	_____	_____	_____
10.	_____	_____	_____

Observation—Knowledge of the Necessity to Make Choices

Date _____

Center/Area _____

Children's Names _____

Ability to Make Wise Choices

Always	**Sometimes**	**Never**
_____	_____	_____

Observation—Concepts of Money or Trading

Date _____

Center/Area _____

Children's Names _____

Accuracy

Not at All	**Some**	**Accurate**
_____	_____	_____

Interview and record children's responses to the following:

1. Pretend it is your birthday. Tell me how you will make a choice between the things you want.
2. Tell me about some of the people who make things that people need.
3. Tell me about some of the people you pay to do things for you that you and your family cannot do (doctor) or do not have time to do (restaurant staff).
4. Tell me about a time when you paid money for something or traded something of yours for another thing.
5. Tell me some of the things that your mother does.

Analyze children's responses for

• completeness

• accuracy

• number of details

11

Living in a Democracy
From Choices to Voting

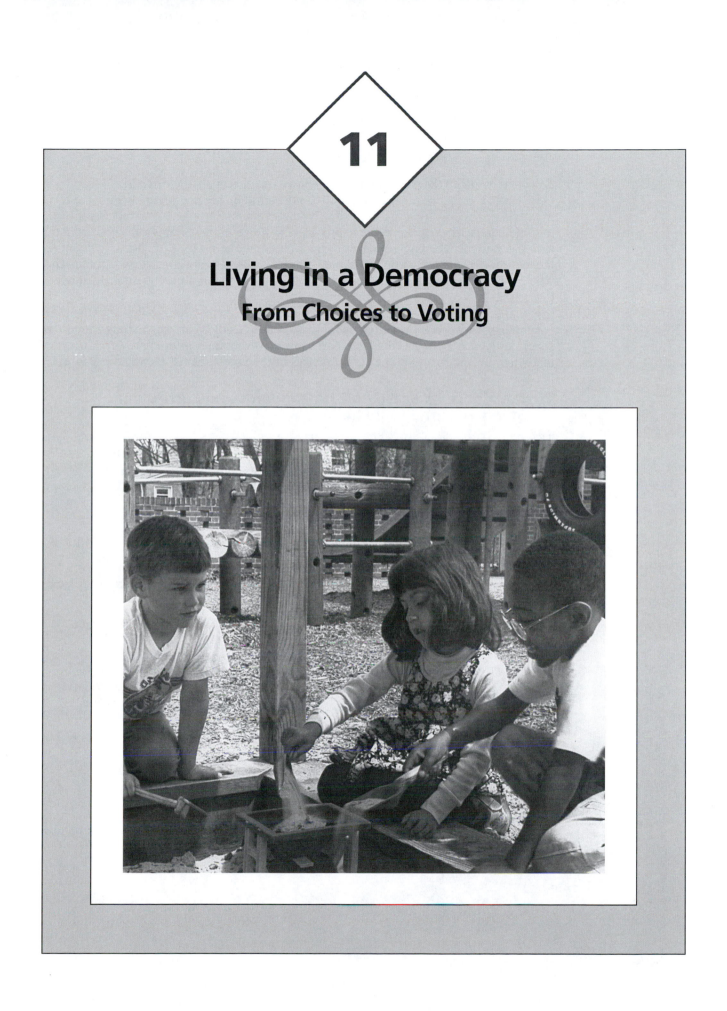

——————————— **FOR THE TEACHER** ———————————

◇ What You'll Need to Know

To vote is to affirm the democratic ideal that we can be responsible for ourselves and participate fully in the welfare of the group. Young children are not yet ready to make all of the decisions necessary to participate in a democratic classroom. Nevertheless, it is important in the early years to begin to provide children with many opportunities to choose and to experience the consequences of their choices. The process of choosing counts in the early years, not the particular choice. For example, it is not important to the teacher whether Collin chooses a book about animals or flowers, but it is of great importance to Collin that he was given his choice.

Children as young as age 3 can make a choice between two possible shirts to wear to school or between a few activities for play. Four-year-olds can pick among alternative snacks or games as long as they get their choice. By the time children are age 5, they are ready to vote and to accept the consequences of the vote—that is, the majority wins.

◇ Key Concepts Based on CTB Standards and Curriculum Standards for Social Studies

The following are related to Civic Ideals and Practices (NCSS, 1994). "In the early grades, students are introduced to civic ideals and practices through activities such as helping to set classroom expectations, examining experiences in relation to ideas, and determining how to balance the needs of individuals and the group" (p. 30).

- Learning to make reasoned choices is prerequisite to voting.

- Making choices means being able to weigh alternatives and listen carefully and critically to the opinions of others.

- When voting, the majority wins, and the consequences of the vote are accepted by the group.

- People vote to establish local, state, and national policies, rules, and leaders.

Children may express their opinions openly and freely and listen to the opinions of others.

◇ **Goals and Objectives**

Children will develop the ability to make choices by choosing their own activities, games, toys, clothes, and books.

Children will be able to express their opinions openly and freely and listen carefully and critically to the opinions of others.

Children will learn to vote as a group and accept the consequences of the group's decision.

Children will assist in establishing classroom expectations.

Children will participate in class meetings.

◇ **What You'll Need**

Making choices, examining and discussing alternatives, and eventually voting on them will be emphasized over the early childhood years and integrated into all areas of the curriculum. Both planned and incidental experiences assist children in the valuing and decision-making process on a continuous basis.

Documents

Young children cannot read the language of the U.S. Constitution and the Bill of Rights, but they should have an opportunity to view copies of those documents and to discuss those parts that involve difficult choices, voting, and voting rights for all people.

Obtain copies of the Declaration of Independence, the Bill of Rights, the Constitution, and other important documents from

The National Archives
Washington, DC 20408
1-800-234-8861
www.nara.gov

The following are two excellent websites for slightly older children: *www. kidsvotingusa.org* and *www.ourdocuments.gov*. Many of the activities and ideas can be adapted for younger children. The latter site provides milestone documents which can be used for discussion.

Reference Books

You may use sections of the following books to illustrate the process of making choices and voting. Older children will not be able to read them alone, but can examine them on their own. Use them to give you some ideas for active experiences.

Fraden, D. B. (1985). *Voting and elections*. Chicago: Children's Press.

Fritz, J. (1987). *Shh! We're writing the Constitution*. New York: G. P. Putnam's Sons.

For younger children,

Bjorkman, S. (1994). *In 1776*. New York: Scholastic.

The following biographies are by D. A. Adler and are published by Holiday, New York:

(1989). *A picture book of Martin Luther King, Jr.*
(1990). *A picture book of Benjamin Franklin.*

(1990). *A picture book of Thomas Jefferson.*

(1991). *A picture book of Eleanor Roosevelt.*

(1996). *A picture book of Patrick Henry.*

Try a book that should be a wonderful motivator for the theme of voting:

Sisulu, E. (1996). *The day Gogo went to vote.* Boston: Little Brown.

Other Things You'll Need

- A copy of "The King's Breakfast" in A. A. Milne's *When We Were Very Young*
- Centers of interest permitting children to make choices
- Large poster paper, flip charts, and drawing tools for recording younger children's choices and older children's votes
- Blocks to depict the number of votes for very young children
- Voting boxes
- Old magazines
- Art materials

The Home-School Connection

Through frequent communications such as the weekly newsletter or a special message, you'll want to ask parents to take their children with them when they go to vote and to explain the process.

Parents will also be encouraged to provide choices for children about their holiday or weekend outings, the clothes they will wear (the night before), foods they will eat (ahead of time), the TV program they will watch, and the games they will play.

You may want to use one of the tear out sheets on pages 162–163 at the end of this chapter or modify them to meet your needs.

◇ Evaluating and Assessing Children's Learning

Assessing children's skills in decision making and voting will be a continuous activity done on an individual and group basis using

- observations
- small- and large-group discussions
- portfolios of children's work
- self-evaluations of children explaining their choices and dictating stories about selections among alternatives and good choices they have made

The tear out sheet on page 164 can be used at different points in the school year to chart growth in children's decision-making skills and understanding of the democratic process of voting.

―――――――――― **FOR THE CHILDREN** ――――――――――

◇ **Standard 1. Children Are Capable of Making Choices**

◆ Provide children with daily opportunities to make choices about the activities they will undertake, the snacks they will eat, and the books they will read. Further, have them participate in class meetings where classroom rules will be examined and discussed. Ask them to

- choose between playing in the shoe store or at the water table

- decide between tapes on African dance and bird sounds

- chose a book to read quietly on their cot before nap time

- pick the color they like best and draw a picture using it

- vote on pudding or applesauce for snack time and record their choices on a chart to see which snack gets the most votes

- measure various things around the classroom with their choice of measuring device

◆ As children play in the activity areas, remind them that they are doing what they chose. When they dictate a story to you about their drawing, remind them that their picture and story are unique. No one told them what to do or how to do it.

◆ When a child is upset because of a poor choice, explain kindly that he or she is not "bad." It was the choice that was at fault. For example, when Jimmy pulled the truck out of Kristin's hands without asking or suggesting a trade, Kristin hit him hard. The teacher of the 4-year-olds explained to Jimmy and Kristin that Jimmy had made a poor choice, but assured them that he would do some "better thinking" next time.

◆ If children are unable to decide what to do, help them to weigh the alternatives. Some children may not be used to making choices for themselves and may ask you, "What should I do?" or "Is this right?" When children really have no ideas, you might offer them two suggestions. If they continue to ask you to decide for them, say "It's entirely up to you. Have you thought of . . . ?" Explain some of the pros

Choice: Pull the truck out of Kristin's hands

Pro	Con
I will get the truck fast	Kristin will cry Kristin may not like me

and cons of each choice. You can make a T-chart to graphically display the advantages and disadvantages of various choices.

Ms. Huang noticed that Ky was very interested in both boats and reptiles. She asked him to help her think about the advantages of making a boat or a snake. Ky decided that the snake was too easy and that he would be more proud of a boat. Ms. Huang told him that she believed he had made a wise decision.

◆   After a walk to look at the flowers growing in the neighborhood, ask children to decide on which flower they liked the best and to tell why. Make a chart of children's preferences along with a brief notation of the reasons for the choice.

When the chart is finished, talk about it. What flower did the group like the best and why? In one kindergarten, the children discovered that buttercups were the favorite because they made pretty yellow marks on their chins.

Ask children to look at the alternative choices: "Blue flowers were popular too. They were chosen seven times." "A lot of you liked marigolds. Look how many of you chose them."

◆   Take a walking trip to a neighborhood food store. Before the walk, ask children to determine how they would collect information about their favorite food. How would they collect data and later display it? They might carry clipboards to permit them to record their choices. They might consider the color, texture, and taste of the food. They would find out if the food is good for children.

Back in the classroom, children could

- make a collage poster of their favorite foods using pictures of food cut from old magazines.

- create a poster of their favorite food using pictures or drawings.

- paint a picture of themselves eating their favorite food.

- prepare speeches to support their favorite food.

- make a graph of their favorite foods along with their explanations for why each was their favorite. This would give them valuable experience in examining alternatives and making choices.

- if the children seemed ready, they would pick a winning food by voting, and the votes would be counted, charted, or graphed.

- finally, make a voting booth out of cardboard and have children enter individually and mark a choice.

◆   You might have a voting party. A vote based on good research and thinking is worth a celebration. Children have collected information on their favorite foods, been to the store to taste and research the nutritional value of them, depicted them in art, and used them in cooking. For literacy, they have prepared short stories and speeches about them. The choices are narrowed to pizza and carrot cake.

- Prepare invitations to send to the families to taste their children's pizza and cake and to enjoy a meal prepared by the school cook.

- After the tasting, encourage the children and their families to use the prepared ballots and ballot box to make their choices between the two alternatives.

- Count the ballots as the children and their families view artwork, stories, speeches, and posters that the children have arranged around the classroom.

- Announce the results. Perhaps pizza wins by a small majority, but both foods have been enjoyed by all.

- Suggest that everyone clap and cheer because in this country we have the right to vote for our choices.

◆ Whenever possible have children choose others for special tasks. You might ask

- one child to choose three other children to go with her or him to take something to the director's office.

- a child to select two other children to work with on a special project.

- children to select four others to sing a part of a song together. When this group finishes, each child selects another to sing another part of the song. Continue until all children have been chosen.

◆ Plan two walking trips around the community. Have the older children vote on their favorite trip by weighing the advantages and disadvantages of each. For example, "At the children's library, we were not allowed to pick the book we wanted to read." "At the bakery, they showed us the big ovens, and we got to taste different kinds of bread and cookies."

◆ Read E. Sisulu's *The Day Gogo Went to Vote* (1996), and ask 5-year-olds to imagine what it would be like if they did not have choices. How would they feel if they were told what to play with and how to play? What would they do if they were told what to paint or build, or which book they were to read?

    Have them make up a short play or puppet show, or make a class book, about how they felt with no choices. Or ask them to plan an activity to illustrate how Gogo and her grandmother must have felt going to vote for the very first time.

◆ Introduce older children to the idea that making choices is difficult and to some of the people who made brave choices in the past. Read David Adler's books about Martin Luther King, Jr.: *Martin Luther King, Jr.: Free at Last,* and *Picture Book of Martin Luther King, Jr.*

    After reading the books, ask children to dictate or write a sentence about a brave choice.

◇ ## Standard 2. What Voting Means

When voting, the majority wins, and the consequences of the vote are accepted by the group. Children who have made many choices for themselves and experienced the consequences of these may be ready to vote and accept the consequences of the vote. Begin voting and learning to accept the consequences by first making sure everyone's choice will be honored. This introduces young children to the idea that not everyone holds the same opinions, but it does not put them in a losing situation.

◆ Ask the class to decide which of two games they want to play. The choices could be between Duck, Duck, Goose and Go In and Out the Window. Each child votes; the group deciding on Duck, Duck plays that game, while the others play the game they selected. You may need an assistant to supervise one of the games.

◆ Read A. A. Milne's "The King's Breakfast" and ask children to taste both marmalade and butter on crackers and decide which is best. Chart their decisions. At snack time, each child gets his or her choice.

◆ Everyday experiences can lead to establishing ongoing class rules as well as changing rules. When boys say to girls, "Girls can't play with blocks," and girls stop trying to enter into block play, it may be a good time to hold a group meeting to discuss class procedures and rules.

Ask the children, both boys and girls, if they think everyone should be able to play with blocks. When children give an opinion, ask them to listen to each other. Ask why—probe children's reasons so they are challenged to really think about their opinions. Make certain that all voices are heard.

Challenge views that are unfair. If children say, "Girls can't build with blocks," you could respond with, "Is that really true? The other day Maria, Casey, and Sabrina built a huge airport that we all admired." After the discussion, ask the class to decide on rules for who should be able to play with the blocks. Post the new rule near the block area.

◆ At group time, ask children to discuss and then vote on

- rules for clean-up time.
- use of towels in the bathroom.
- what specific equipment they want to use outside on a given day.
- whose turn it is to complete room tasks or roles such as caring for classroom animals and plants.
- what safety rules will be used for a specific piece of playground equipment.

These rules may be modified as the children discuss how well the rules are working. Through active participation in making their own choices and voting on rules, they realize how important such documents are to the management of the classroom and society.

◆ Ask children to imagine what their classroom would be like if there were no rules.

Voting and following the will of the majority prepares children for their role as citizens of a democracy.

◇ **Standard 3. Why People Vote**

People vote to establish local, state, and national policies, rules, and leaders. However, voting and making choices are an integral part of everyday life and need not be connected to a publicized local or national election. Of course, you'll want to capitalize on election times to make the process concrete for young children through direct experiences.

◆ Arrange the book corner with stories and reference books that reflect the themes of democracy, history and biography, equality, and cooperation. Encourage children to use the methods of the historian in consulting them for assistance in making choices and voting.

◆ After reading D. A. Adler's *A Picture Book of Thomas Jefferson* (1990), you could place hats and costumes representative of the Revolutionary period, documents, voting boxes, paper and markers, and poster board in the dramatic area for 5-year-olds. Children could create posters for candidates and cut paper for ballots. Or they could make a "constitution" for the playground.

◆ Ask parents to take their children with them when they vote. After they do so, provide props for the creative dramatic corner that would encourage choices and voting as themes for sociodramatic play.

◇ **Reflecting**

Have children *apply* their knowledge of making choices and voting.

◆ Read D. A. Adler's *A Picture Book of Benjamin Franklin* (1990). Ask the children to describe what choices Franklin made and why he thought it was important for people to vote. Have the children describe what life would be like if they did not have their choice of leaders, if one or more people told everyone else what to do. How would life change? Would they have to do what they were told?

◆ Read D. A. Adler's *A Picture Book of Martin Luther King, Jr.* (1989). Ask the children to describe what life was like for African Americans before they were accorded the vote and other rights. How would it feel not to be able to go to the pool, or to any restaurant or store? Why is it important that we do not allow these rights to be taken away? How can we prevent these rights from being taken away?

◇ **Extending and Expanding to the Early Primary Grades**

Early primary-age children can do the following activities:

◆ Participate in running a democratic classroom. From setting the rules to having frequent discussions about how they are working, to formulating new rules, they may gradually assume responsibility for most aspects of classroom life. Children experience governing themselves rather than memorizing easily forgotten information about government.

◆ Consider the needs of the group by perspective taking. Provide many opportunities for children to listen to the perspectives of others by giving them a common experience such as viewing pictures of the civil rights movement, and then providing the opportunity for them to express and defend their perspectives of the experience to each other.

◆ Research and learn about historical events that are of interest to them. A very good reference book for teachers is J. Hakem's *All the People* (1995). The book is part of a series, *A History of Us,* and is designed for "young people from 9 to 99." Another more recent book is M. S. Turck's *The Civil Rights Movement for Kids: A History with 21 Activities* (2000). Using these books, you may want to pose problems for the children:

- "How would you feel if you were one of three African American boys and six African American girls that integrated Central High in Little Rock for the first time? Some people threw rocks at them and used nasty words." Let the children make a class book reflecting the discussion.

- "How would you feel if you couldn't vote because you were a woman?"

- "Suppose you didn't believe in war. What would you do if our country entered a war that you didn't believe in? March? Wear a black armband? Go to jail?"

- "You have been running your classroom. Why do you think it is sometimes necessary to have a court make a final decision?"

◆ Practice empathy and social responsibility. First you may have children do this in the classroom as facilitators for disabled children or different-language speakers. Buddies are helpful for new children in school. Then generalize it to the wider community. Have the children read about and view pictures and videos about poverty and homelessness. Many will have observed homeless persons in their neighborhoods. Elicit their suggestions for helping less fortunate persons. Have a vote and put some plans into action. Each child may choose a way to become a community helper.

◆ Make connections to their school administration and their local and national governments. Children may generate issues with which they agree or disagree. They can write to the principal about better facilities for developmentally different children or to the mayor about cleaning up the park. The possibilities are endless. You may want to make sure they have researched and supported their position.

◇ Documenting Children's Learning

A web can document the learning, skills, and attitudes children gained through voting and choice making. Hang the web in a place where it can be seen by visitors as well as the children. Add an explanation such as "This year we have learned to vote and make decisions. We are beginning to understand what democracy means. These are some of the things we have learned." You will also want to display photographs of the children that you have taken as they participated in the various activities. Voting and following the will of the majority prepare children for their role as citizens of a democracy.

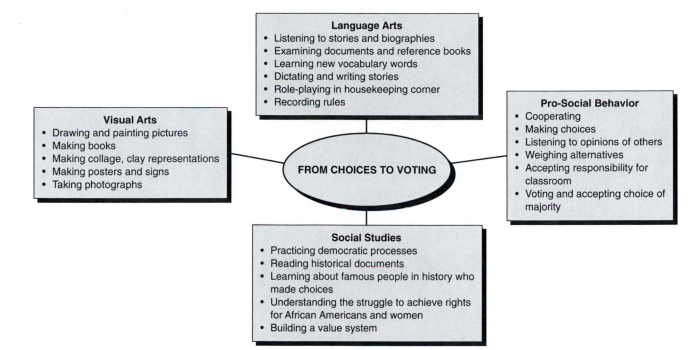

Date _____

Dear Parents:

As part of our curriculum, we are working on helping your children to make choices. We want them to provide reasons for their choices, and eventually to vote on their preferences by examining alternatives. As the year progresses, they will be participating more and more in sharing decision making about classroom rules. We also expect them to cooperate and accept responsibility for the classroom.

Since you are your child's most important teacher, we need your help! Will you provide your children with the opportunity to make choices about the things they will do? Since they are young, you may want to limit the choices to two or three possibilities. An example would be which book they would like to read with you at bedtime.

As you know, elections are in November. Please take your children with you to vote and explain the process to them. Let them talk to the people outside the polling places and examine the buttons and materials they hand out. If you are not eligible to vote, there are meetings and other opportunities for your children to experience the voting process.

Sincerely,

Date _____

Dear Parents:

We want to welcome you to a very special event at school. Your whole family is invited, and transportation will be provided for anyone who needs it. Just drop us a note. On _____ at _____ in the _____ at school, we will be having a voting party. As you know, your children have been collecting information about their favorite foods. They have also been making posters to represent these foods, and preparing short speeches to persuade others to vote for their food.

The class has narrowed down the choices, and we have been to the neighborhood store to buy the favorites. We will have plenty of food on hand for all of us to sample (and more prepared by our wonderful cook). There will be a vote, and we will count the votes and chart the results.

In preparing for this event, your children have been making choices by examining the alternatives and listening to the ideas of others. They have been participating in a democratic process.

We thank you so much for working with us and look forward to seeing you.

Sincerely,

Date _____

Name of Child _____

Age of Child _____

Individual Evaluation: Evaluating and Assessing Children's Skills at Making Choices and Voting

	Always	Sometimes	Never
Actively participates in choosing among alternatives.	_____	_____	_____
Is able to provide reasons for choices.	_____	_____	_____
Expresses opinions appropriately.	_____	_____	_____
Listens to opinions of others.	_____	_____	_____
Cooperates with others in setting and following rules.	_____	_____	_____
Uses vocabulary appropriate to new concepts.	_____	_____	_____
Can follow the will of the majority.	_____	_____	_____
Demonstrates an ability to think critically about choices.	_____	_____	_____
Stands up for what he/she thinks is right.	_____	_____	_____
Demonstrates an understanding of why people must make brave choices.	_____	_____	_____
Demonstrates some understanding of choices and voting in U.S. history.	_____	_____	_____

12

Valuing Diversity

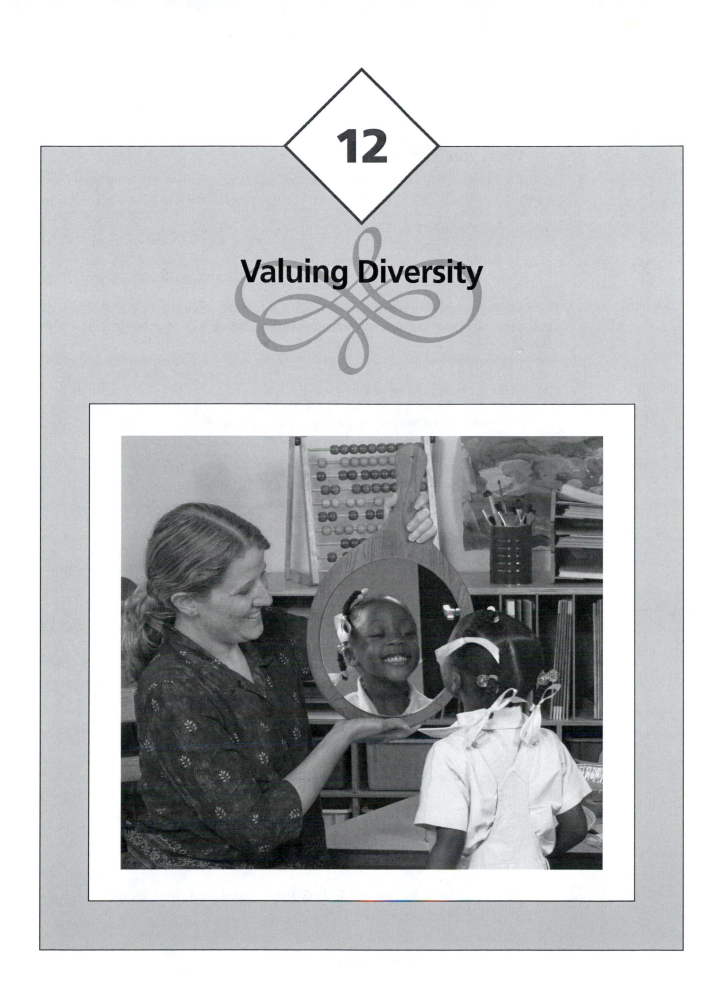

─── FOR THE TEACHER ───

◇ What You'll Need to Know

Some think that children are born without prejudices and learn to prejudge others who differ from them through interactions with their parents and the larger society. The media and a community's values, whether subtle or overt, certainly convey a great deal of information to children.

Yet young children, through their egocentric eyes, may respond negatively to individuals and things that possess unfamiliar characteristics. Much to the dismay of Dr. Simmons, a well-known psychologist, his 4-year-old daughter yelled in a shopping mall, "I can't believe that man has no leg. He is so ugly."

Mr. Fortier, the teacher of the 3-year-olds, believed it was necessary to challenge the prejudices in young children when he overheard a group talking about Tiffany's dirty skin. Renaldo suggested that they could get rid of the dark color if they "washed her a lot." The teacher had also heard some boys in the housekeeping center insist that they shouldn't have to take care of the babies. And then there was the time that Karen called Sophia stupid because Sophia knew few English words. Mr. Fortier reasoned, as good teachers would, that if he did nothing for these children, the result would be racism, sexism, and stereotypes about those with developmental differences. He wanted the children in his classroom to value and care for each other.

Teaching children to value diversity is not an easy task for teachers. It requires that young children experience a multifaceted, antibias curriculum each day they enter the classroom. The antibias classroom actively challenges prejudice, stereotyping, bias, and negative decisions made about persons on the basis of race, ethnicity, language, gender, and ability.

An excellent source for the teacher is: Bullard, S., Carnes, J., Hofer, M., Polk, N., and Hernandez Sheets, R. (1997). *Starting small: Teaching tolerance in preschool and the early grades.* Montgomery, AL: Southern Poverty Law Center, Teaching Tolerance Project. This book comes in video form as well.

Also check Schniedewind, N., & Davidson, E. (1998). *Open minds to equality: A sourcebook of learning activities to affirm diversity and promote equity.* Boston: Allyn and Bacon, and Byrnes, D.A., & Kiger, G. (Eds.). (1996). *Common bonds: Anti-bias teaching in a diverse society.* Wheaton, MD: ACEI.

A more recent book that will prove invaluable in assisting you with teaching in a multicultural, multilingual society, promoting gender equity, forging a caring classroom community, and promoting gender equity is: Copple, C. (Ed.). (2003). *A world of difference.* Washington, DC: NAEYC.

Although meant for older children, the teacher may consult for ideas: Turck, M. C. (2000). *The civil rights movement for kids: A history with 21 activities.* Chicago: Chicago Review Press.

For children's books, check the Caldecott (*www.ala.org/alsc/caldecott.html*) and Coretta Scott King (*www.ala.org/snt/csking*) award winners online. The Coretta Scott King Task Force of the American Library Association's Ethnic Multicultural Information Exchange Round Table picks the Coretta Scott King awardees. The authors and illustrators must be of African descent. Their books promote an understanding and appreciation of the "American Dream."

◇ Key Concepts Based on CTB Guidelines and Curriculum Standards for Social Studies

- Racial/ethnic awareness, which starts with the identification of physical characteristics and ethnic values, customs, and language styles, and ends with respect for others (Domain 1, Self-Knowledge, Social Skills, and Motivation to Learn, Guideline 1, Children Will Develop Knowledge of Self, Guideline 2, Children Will Develop Knowledge of Others and Social Skills, CTB; Theme I, Culture, Theme IV, Individual Development and Identity, and Theme IX, Global Connections, Curriculum Standards for Social Studies).

- Awareness and respect for persons with diverse abilities. Children appear to begin with curiosity about unusual attributes of persons and the special equipment they need. Later they want to know more about what such persons can and cannot do, and finding them lacking in some physical or cognitive area, may develop biases against them that must be countered (see previous text).

- Gender awareness and respect for the equality of persons of both genders. Between the ages of 4 and 7, children come to realize that being male and being female are permanent biological conditions. At the same time, they begin to learn the expectations associated with gender roles and to act these out in classroom play. These, too, must be countered (see previous text).

◇ Goals and Objectives

Children will read and appreciate stories depicting children and adults of all ethnic groups; enjoy art, music, and games of other cultures; and play with children whose ethnicity/race differs from their own.

Children will play with children with special needs, involving them in their group work, games, and activities.

Children will play equally with boys and girls and pick toys on the basis of choice, not gender.

Critically, children will challenge stereotypes they find in books, toys, greeting cards, or television programs.

Children will practice fairness and justice in cooperating with all members of their class.

◇ What You'll Need

The valuing of diversity will be developed over the early childhood years and integrated into all areas of the curriculum. In teaching children to value diversity, the classroom environment is crucial. The following will be important in setting the stage and in allowing children to experience an antibias classroom:

- Evaluate your materials. For example, make sure that you have plenty of brown paint in your art center and dolls of both genders and various racial and ethnic groups in your dramatic play area. Another good idea is to have multicultural skin color crayons available.  Are your props free of items that stereotype, such as "Indian" headdresses and sombreros? Are children's books free of stereotypes? Do manipulatives reflect diversity? Does the music you use reflect a variety of cultures?

- Examine your environment. Are equipment and materials adaptable to differently abled children (and staff)? Are inside and outside environments barrier-free? Do they provide enough variety so that all children will have challenging activities?

Are the walls filled with images that accurately reflect the diversity of life in the United States? For example, are a variety of family styles depicted?

Children's Books

Before choosing books for the antibias classroom, you may want to devise some criteria for selecting literature that promotes respect for all. Consider the following points:

- Are characters portrayed as individuals without stereotyping?

- Would the book qualify as good literature regardless of its focus?

- Do the illustrations or photographs contain accurate, authentic portraits of people and scenes from different cultural and gender groups as well as persons who are developmentally different?

- Do the characters speak in a style and language that fits their situation?

- Are various lifestyles represented fairly and respectfully?

- Do characters have the ability to solve problems and have power over their life choices?

The following are among the many good books that promote the valuing of diversity and fairness in young children:

DISABILITIES

dePaola, T. (1981). *Now one foot, now the other.* New York: Putnam. When a young boy's grandfather has a stroke, the boy teaches him to relearn walking.

DIVERSITY AND DISABILITY

Martin, B., Jr. (1987). *Knots on a counting rope.* New York: Henry Holt. A Native American man ties knots on a rope to mark the growing self-confidence of his blind grandson.

GENDER AND DIVERSITY

Hoffman, M. (1991). *Amazing Grace.* New York: Dial. An African American girl believes she can be Peter Pan in the school play.

DIVERSITY AND PREJUDICE

Rappoport, D. (2002). *Martin's big words.* New York: Hyperion. Listening to his father preach, the great civil rights leader vows that he will get "big words" too.
Ringgold, F. (1999). *If a bus could talk: The story of Rosa Parks.* New York: Simon and Schuster. A talking bus relates the story of Rosa Parks, who refused to give up her seat in the front of the bus and thereby triggered the Montgomery Bus Boycott.

MULTICULTURALISM

Say, A. (1994). *My grandfather's journey.* New York: Houghton. The author's family history illustrates the mixed emotions involved in immigration and acculturation.

CULTURE AND SOCIAL CLASS

Ringgold, F. (1991). *Tar beach.* New York: Crown. The roof of her Harlem apartment building is Cassie's beach front from which she flies to help her father find work.

NATIVE AMERICAN

Morgan, W. (Ed.). (1988). *Navajo coyote tales.* Santa Fe, New Mexico: Ancient City Press. First published by the Bureau of Indian Affairs. Translated and adapted in English.

Music for an Antibias Music Program

The joy and sorrow of singing, dancing, and marching to the music of the civil rights movement inspire children to value diversity. There are also a large number of songs from other cultures and in other languages. The following songbooks are recommended:

Bryan, A. (1974). *Walk together children, black American spirituals.* New York: Atheneum.

Cooper, F. (1998). *Cumbayah.* New York: Morrow Junior Books.

Krull, K. (1992). *Gonna sing my head off! American folk songs for children.* New York: Alfred A. Knopf, Inc.

Raschka, C. (1992). *Charlie Parker played be bop.* New York: Orchard Books.

Yurchenco, H. (Ed.). (1967). *A fiesta of folk songs from Spain and Latin America.* New York: G. P. Putnam's Sons.

Song tapes or CDs by Ella Jenkins, Joan Baez, Bob Dylan, and Judy Collins emphasize the huge struggles involved in developing respect for diversity.

Video

Follow the Drinking Gourd shows a young girl and her family escaping from slavery via the Underground Railroad (Rabbit Ears Video). It can also be found in book form.

Websites

Department of Justice Web Page for Children (*www.usdoj.gov/kidspage/bias-k-5/index.htm*)

Smithsonian National Museum of the American Indian (*www.AmericanIndian.si.edu*)

Other Resources

- Puzzles, small manipulatives, and props for the creative dramatic corner that depict persons of diverse racial and ethnic backgrounds. Materials should be balanced by gender and accessible to those with developmental disabilities.

- Art supplies and papers reflecting the colors of various racial and ethnic groups.

- Pictures and photographs depicting various cultures displayed around the room.

- Full-length and handheld mirrors for children to begin to form a racial/ethnic identity.

- Signs and posters in the various languages spoken in the classroom.

A photograph documents that children value each other and form friendships.

The Home-School Connection

As you continuously work with children in creating a classroom that celebrates diversity, you will want to ask parents to support your goals at home. This should not be viewed as parent education, but as an interchange of ideas between parents and the school. Disagreements may be inevitable, but will be kept at a minimum if parents are treated with respect and invited to participate in curriculum development, implementation, and evaluation. Written communications with parents should reflect the languages spoken in the home.

You may want to use one of the tear out sheets on pages 176–177 at the end of this chapter or modify them to meet your needs.

◇ Evaluating and Assessing Children's Learning

Assessing children's progress in valuing diversity will be a continuous activity done on an individual and group basis using observations, portfolios, and structured interviews with individual children. Observe children's play and interactions over a period of time. Are there indications that children are being excluded because of their characteristics? What toys are boys and girls playing with? Evaluate your own interactions with children. Are you modeling the behavior you want from the children in your classroom?

The evaluation on the tear out sheet on page 178 may be used at different points in the school year.

——————————————— **FOR THE CHILDREN** ———————————————

◇ Standard 1. Valuing Cultural Diversity

Activities are designed to encourage children to observe, gather data, and organize it for interpretation.

◆ Take pictures of the children in your group, and ask parents to send in photographs of the family. Fill a large bulletin board with them or place them in different centers. Encourage children to view the pictures and discuss what is the same and what is different about the persons depicted.

After children have discussed what is the same and what is different about the children in the class and their families, organize the data that the children have observed by making a T-chart listing what is the same and what is different about the pictures.

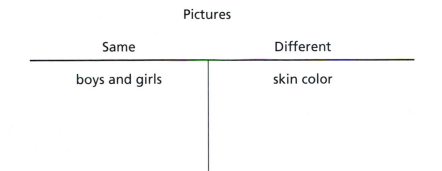

Pictures

Same	Different
boys and girls	skin color

◆ Place a few full-length mirrors in the housekeeping corner. When one or two children are playing there, ask them questions about their skin, eye, and hair color as they look at themselves and others: "Do you know what color your eyes are, Anthony?" "What color eyes does Katie have?" You may find out what they know and also the value they attach to it. If Anthony replies that he has black eyes, but Katie's blue ones are "better and nicer," you will need to help them to understand that different is not better.

◆ As children play with art materials, comment on the skin shades the children are using in their pictures.

◆ Suggest that children look in the mirror and create a self-portrait. Comment on the lovely colors they are using. Either informally with young children or during large-group meeting time with older children, compare self-portraits.

◆ Read M. Hoffman's *Amazing Grace* (1991). Discuss why the children in the book believed that Grace could not be Peter Pan because of her skin color and gender. Have them dictate sentences about why that turned out to be wrong.

◆ Play tapes from the civil rights movement and read Faith Ringgold's *If a Bus Could Talk: The Story of Rosa Parks* (1999). Ask the children how they would feel if they could not go to the swimming pool or ride in the front of the bus because of their skin color.

◆ Discuss the illustrations in Faith Ringgold's book *Tar Beach* (1991). The children will notice the quilt motif. Discuss why the quilts were so important in the African American experience. Have the children each make a quilt square depicting what is important to them about themselves or their families. These can be as simple as squares of paper. Put the pieces together to create a classroom quilt. Note: Quilts are important to American Indians as well. You might do the same activity with the emphasis on American Indians.

◆ Teach children simple songs and dances in different languages. Use these as a basis for a planned activity for parents.

◆ Put up posters by famous artists of different cultures. Have the children compare color, use of media, and line. Have them dictate a story about how each work of art makes them feel. A good book to exhibit in the classroom is about the African American artist Romare Bearden. There are large pictures of his collages and artwork. A good resource is Sims' *Romare Bearden* (1993).

◆ Invite a family or community member to demonstrate the pottery or weaving typical of his or her culture. Make sure children are prepared in advance to ask questions and have materials on hand so that they may actively practice the skills they have learned.

◆ Create a minimuseum with artifacts that the children have brought from home reflecting different cultures. These may include stamps, dolls, foods, items of dress, and toys. Have children visit the museum in small groups, and dictate a story about their visit.

◆ Take walking trips to different ethnic neighborhoods. Have children describe and record the activities that took place, any unique characteristics of the buildings, and the sounds and smells.

◇ **Standard 2. Valuing Others with Special Needs**

◆ Read B. Martin, Jr's *Knots on a Counting Rope* (1987). Ask children to close their eyes and pretend what it might be like to be blind. Would they fear having a friend who is blind? How would they arrange the room so a blind friend could play without help?

Children with special needs master advanced skills with help from persons who value their potential.

◆ Make lists of things that people with disabilities can and can't do. Take a research walk around the school and find out if it is accessible to all children. For example, are the bathrooms, water fountains, and doorknobs at the right level for children in wheelchairs? Make a KWHL chart. It should look like this:

Topic/Question: Are school facilities accessible to all children?

K What I know	W What I want to learn	H How I will learn it	L What I learned
	Is water fountain accessible?	Research walk	Water fountain is not accessible

◆ Have differently abled children identify games and activities in which everyone can participate. Encourage children to try one of these games each day. Have children discuss how they could modify games to make them inclusive.

◆ Read T. dePaola's *Now One Foot, Now the Other* (1981). Discuss with children why time and patience are often needed to assist persons who have, or have had, a serious illness.

◇ Standard 3. Valuing Gender Equality

◆ Support children's exploration of nonstereotypic gender roles. If Carol says, "Boys can't feed the baby," counter the stereotype and help boys get involved in dramatic play.

◆ Make sure the girls have access to the block area as well as the trucks and cars. Support their play.

◆ Invite a parent who has a nonstereotypical work role to talk to the children. Make sure they are prepared with questions to ask.

◆ Using recycled magazines, have children make a collage of workers in nonstereotypic jobs.

◆ Discuss with children what type of work they would like to do. Make a Venn Diagram. Compare boys' choices with girls' choices. See where they overlap. If the choices are stereotypic, help children to list the duties of each job and determine if both males and females could fulfill them. Continue to counter the stereotypes with "why?" and "why not?" questions.

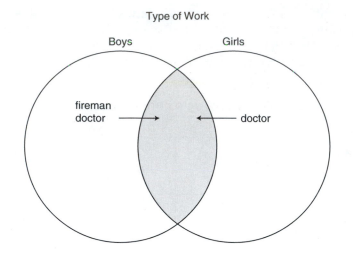

Type of Work

◇ **Reflecting and Reaching Conclusions**

◆   Have children make graphs of the eye and skin colors represented in the classroom. Read K. Kissinger's *All the Colors We Are/Todos Los Colores de Puestra Piel,* which explains in simple language (English and Spanish) and through photographs how we got our skin color. Have children dictate stories about skin color.

◆   Begin to critique books, toys, greeting cards, and television programs for stereotypes. Have children look for diversity in a bookstore or toy store. In the drugstore, Molly noticed that there were no cards that depicted African American children. She reasoned that they would feel bad if they came to buy a card.

◇ **Extending and Expanding to the Early Primary Grades**

Primary-age children can do the following:

◆   Think critically about fairness and justice. Mr. Barton, the second-grade teacher, helped the children to make a book about race/ethnicity, gender, and visible disabilities with "fair" and "unfair" pictures on facing pages. Children were urged to locate pictures in magazines and catalogs from stores. Under each picture, children wrote a few sentences about why the picture was fair or unfair. Ilene arrived one morning with her brother's "Indian warrior" and said, "It's unfair. Let's throw it out."

◆   Critique books on the basis of gender equity. Bring in an older book that depicts strict gender roles in appearance and behavior. Have the children decide whether it reflects the abilities of males and females.

◆   Take field trips more easily than younger children. Visit ethnic neighborhoods and sample the foods. Visit a toy store and have the children take an inventory of toys that are biased and unbiased.

◆   Record their critiques of TV programs and commercials. While it is desirable for children to watch pro-social programming on TV, you might plan to have the children watch a program that is biased. Have children notice how characters are depicted. Are they representative of the racial/ethnic group or stereotypic? What about the language? Do all Hispanics talk that way? What about the surroundings? Are all African Americans poor?

◆ Conduct research. Have children research the origins of their names. Names may originate for various reasons based on race and culture. The children can talk with their parents and/or use research books. This project may culminate in a Name Book that includes the research findings of each class member and a picture of the author.

◆ Employ creative writing as a learning tool. Have the class create a group poem on the theme of valuing diversity.

◆ Understand maps and globes. Be sure that these are available in the classroom for children to locate their country of origin. Children may put a pin with their name attached on a map at the spot where their family originated.

◆ Understand fairness and justice. Use group meetings to discuss fairness. Create a setting that is conducive to talking and listening. Have the children draft rules to live by in the classroom that value diversity in all of its forms. Try them for a while, and evaluate them with the children. Ask the children if they need to be modified.

◆ Challenge stereotypes. Are all black people great athletes? How can we find out if this is true?

◇ Documenting Children's Learning

A web can document the learning, skills, and attitudes children gained through their exposure to a classroom that emphasizes valuing and celebrating diversity.

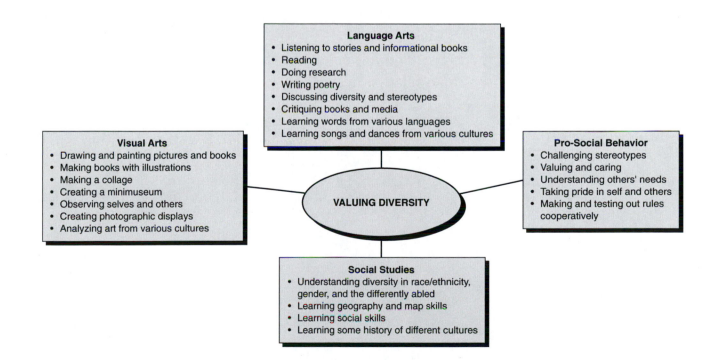

Date _____

Dear Parents:

As part of our curriculum, we are working on an antibias classroom. By this, we mean a classroom where all children and their families are equally valued. Our goals include justice and fairness for all racial/ethnic groups, boys and girls, and children who are developmentally different. Since it is the beginning of the school year, we are asking you to provide some information, because you are the most important resource and source of information about your child.

As you have time, could you bring or send us the answers to these questions?

- What would you like to teach your child about racial/ethnic identity, disabilities, or being a girl or a boy?

- What experiences have your children had with persons different from themselves?

- Have you discussed race, developmental differences, or gender differences with your child? If so, what have you talked about?

- Will you listen to comments your child may make about differences based upon race, language, or gender? If you could keep a small journal, we would love to know what he or she says at home.

- Do you have pictures or other items that represent your culture that you could lend us for a short period of time? If so, we will be sure to share them with the children.

If you have time to join us in the classroom, please feel welcome. Just let us know when you are coming and if you have something special you would like to share or do with the children.

Sincerely,

Permission is granted by the publisher to reproduce this page.

176

Date _____

Dear Parents:

We want to welcome you and your children (siblings too) to a very special occasion at school. On _____ at _____, we will be having a Family Night Out in the _____, featuring a special dinner.

We will be playing the music you sent in from various cultures, and the children will sing some songs as well. Children's work will be exhibited for you to see.

Then, we will have a parent meeting and discussion. Baby-sitting will be provided for your other children. The staff of the center and a family social worker will be on hand to discuss the development of children's concepts about race, gender, and children who are developmentally different. We will focus on how teachers and parents can work together to build a strong sense of identity in the child. Then, we will be available to answer your questions.

Please join us for this wonderful evening event. We look forward to greeting you.

Sincerely,

Date _____

Group Evaluation

For 3-year-olds and older:

	Always	Sometimes	Never
• When appropriate, do children show pride about their race/ethnic group?	_____	_____	_____
• When appropriate, do children show pride in their gender identity?	_____	_____	_____
• Do children play with children with developmental differences?	_____	_____	_____
• Do children demonstrate an awareness of the commonalities among people?	_____	_____	_____
• Do children demonstrate an understanding of the differences among people?	_____	_____	_____

For 4-year-olds and older:

	Always	Sometimes	Never
• Do children demonstrate an ability to think critically about stereotypes in books, television, cards, and toys?	_____	_____	_____
• Do children demonstrate an ability to challenge stereotypes when children or teachers express them in the classroom?	_____	_____	_____
• Are children able to make rules that reflect caring and justice?	_____	_____	_____

• What mechanisms seem most effective in helping children to value diversity:

	Always	Sometimes	Never
Children's books	_____	_____	_____
Art projects	_____	_____	_____
Informal discussions	_____	_____	_____
Formal discussions	_____	_____	_____
Dramatic play	_____	_____	_____
Teacher-directed lessons	_____	_____	_____
Field experiences	_____	_____	_____
Other	_____	_____	_____

References

Ada, A. F. (2003). *A magical encounter: Latino children's literature in the classroom.* Boston, MA: Allyn & Bacon.

Alexander, K. L., & Entwisle, D. R. (1988). Achievement in the first 2 years of school: Patterns and processes. *Monographs of the Society for Research in Child Development, 53*(2), Serial No. 288.

Beaty, J. J. (1997). *Building bridges with multicultural picture books for children 3–5.* Upper Saddle River, NJ: Prentice Hall.

Berk, L. E., & Winsler, A. (1995). *Scaffolding children's learning: Vygotsky and early childhood education.* Washington, DC: NAEYC.

Bisgaier, C. S., & Samaras, T. (2004). Using wood, glue, and words to enhance learning. *Young Children, 59,* 22–29.

Blaska, J. K., & Lynch, E. C. (1998). Is everyone included? Using children's literature to facilitate the understanding of disabilities. *Young Children, 53,* 36–40.

Bodrova, E., & Leong, D. J. (2003). Building language and literacy through play. *Early Childhood Today, 18,* 34–40.

Box, J. A., & Little, D. C. (2003). Cooperative small-group instruction combined with advanced organizers and their relationship to self-concept and social studies achievement of elementary school students. *Journal of Instructional Psychology, 30,* 49–56.

Bredekamp, S. (1998). *Tools for teaching developmentally appropriate practice: The leading edge in early childhood education.* Washington, DC: NAEYC.

Bredekamp, S. (2003). Resolving contradictions between cultural practices. In C. Copple (Ed.), *A world of difference: Readings on teaching young children in a diverse society* (pp. 59–60). Washington, DC: NAEYC.

Bredekamp, S., & Copple, C. (1997). *Developmentally appropriate practice in early childhood programs* (rev. ed.). Washington, DC: NAEYC.

Bredekamp, S., & Rosegrant, T. (1995). *Reaching potentials: Transforming early childhood curriculum and assessment* (Vol. 2). Washington, DC: NAEYC.

Bronfenbrenner, U. (1979). *The ecology of human development: Experiments by nature and design.* Cambridge, MA: Harvard University Press.

Bronson, M. B. (1995). *The right stuff.* Washington, DC: NAEYC.

Bruner, J. (1966). *Toward a theory of instruction.* Cambridge, MA: Belknap/Harvard.

Byrnes, D. A., & Kiger, G. (Eds.). Common bonds: Anti-bias teaching in a diverse society. Wheaton, MD: ACEI.

Casbergue, R. M., & Kieff, J. (1998). Marbles anyone? Traditional games in the classroom. *Childhood Education, 74,* 143–147.

Cassidy, D. J., Mims, S., & Rucker, L. (2003). Emergent curriculum and kindergarten readiness. *Childhood Education, 79,* 194–199.

Chalufour, I., & Worth, K. (2004). *Building structures with young children.* St. Paul, MN: Redleaf Press.

Charlesworth, R., Hart, C. H., Burts, D. C., & DeWolf, M. (1993). The LSU studies: Building a research base for developmentally appropriate practice. In S. Reifel (Ed.), *Perspectives on developmentally appropriate practice: Advances in early education and daycare* (Vol. 5, pp. 3–28). Greenwich, CT: JEI Press.

Clay, J. W. (2004). Creating safe, just places to learn for children of lesbian and gay parents. *Young Children, 59,* 34–38.

Colker, L. (2005). *The cooking book: Fostering young children's learning and delight.* Washington, DC: NAEYC.

Commume di Reggio Emilia. (1987). *To make a portrait of a lion.* Reggio Emilia, Italy: Author.

Cooper, J., & Dever, M. T. (2001). Socio-dramatic play as a vehicle for curriculum integration in first grade. *Young Children, 56,* 58–63.

Copple, C. (Ed.). (2003). *A world of difference: Readings on teaching young children in a diverse society.* Washington, DC: NAEYC.

CTB. (2003). *Pre-Kindergarten Standards: Guidelines for teaching and learning.* Monterey, CA. CTB/McGraw-Hill.

Derman-Sparks, L. (2003). Markers of multicultural/antibias education. In C. Copple (Ed.), *A world of difference: Readings on teaching young children in a diverse society* (pp. 171–172). Washington, DC: NAEYC.

Dewey, J. (1900). *The school and society.* Chicago: University of Chicago Press.

Dewey, J. (1938). *Experience and education.* New York: Collier Books.

Dewey, J. (1944). *Democracy and education.* New York: The Free Press.

Diamond, K. E., & Stacey, S. (2003). The other children at preschool: Experiences of typically developing children in inclusive programs. In C. Copple (Ed.), *A world of difference: Readings on teaching young children in a diverse society* (pp. 135–139). Washington, DC: NAEYC.

Dighe, J., Calomiris, Z., & Van Zutphen, C. (1998). Nurturing the language of art in children. *Young Children, 53,* 4–9.

Dyson, A. H. (1988). The value of time off task: Young children's spontaneous talk and deliberate text. *Harvard Educational Review, 97,* 396–420.

Feeney, S., & Freeman, N. K. (1999). *Ethics and the early childhood educator: Using the NAEYC Code.* Washington, DC: NAEYC.

Gardner, H. (1993). *Frames of mind: The theory of multiple intelligences.* New York: Basic Books.

Georgetown University Child Development Center. (1989). Toward a culturally competent system of care. Washington, DC: Author.

Gesell, A., Ilg, F., & Ames, L. B. (1974). *Infant and child in the culture of today.* New York: Harper & Row.

Goleman, D. (1995). *Emotional intelligence.* New York: Bantam Books.

Grolnick, W. S., & Slowiaczek, M. L. (1994). Parents' involvement in children's schooling: A multi-dimensional conceptualization and motivational model. *Child Development, 65,* 237–252.

Hakem, J. (1995). *All the people.* New York: Oxford University Press.

Hirsch, E. S., (Ed.). (1996). *The block book.* Washington, DC: NAEYC.

Honigman, J. J., & Bhavnagri, N. P. (1998). Painting with scissors: Art education beyond production. *Childhood Education, 74,* 205–213.

Katz, L. (1993). What can we learn from Reggio Emilia? In C. Edwards, L. Gandini, and G. Forman (Eds.), *The hundred languages of children* (pp. 19–41). Norwood, NJ: Ablex.

Katz, L. (1998). *The leading edge.* Washington, DC: NAEYC.

Kaufman, H. O. (2003). Skills for working with all families. In C. Copple (Ed.), *A world of difference: Readings on teaching young children in a diverse society.* Washington, DC. Author.

Kemple, K. M., Batey, J. J., & Hartle L. C. (2004). Music play: Creating centers for musical play and exploration. *Young Children, 59,* 30–37.

Kreeger Museum. (2004). *Kreeger Museum School Tour: Nature through art.* Washington, DC: Author.

Levin, D. E. (2000). Learning about the world through play. *Early Childhood Today, 15,* 56–67.

Loughlin, C., & Suina, J. (1982). *The learning environment: An instructional strategy.* New York: Teachers College Press.

Mallory, B. L. (1998). Educating young children with developmental differences: Principles of inclusive practice. In C. Seefeldt & A. Galper (Eds.), *Continuing issues in early childhood education* (2nd ed., pp. 213–237). Upper Saddle River NJ: Merrill/Prentice Hall.

Mallory, B. L., & New, R. S. (1994). *Diversity and developmentally appropriate practices: Challenges to early childhood education.* New York: Teachers College Press.

Marcon, R. A. (1992). Differential effects of three preschool models on inner-city 4-year olds. *Early Childhood Research Quarterly, 7,* 517–530.

Marion, M. (1995). *Guidance of young children* (4th ed.). Upper Saddle River, NJ: Merrill/ Prentice Hall.

Maryland State Department of Education. (1992). *Laying the foundation for school success: Recommendations for improving early learning programs.* Baltimore, MD: Author.

Matlock, R., & Hornstein, J. (2004). Sometimes a smudge is just a smudge, and sometimes it's a saber-toothed tiger: Learning and the arts through the ages. *Young Children, 59,* 12–17.

McAfee, O., & Leong, D. (2001). *Assessing and guiding young children's development and learning.* New York: Allyn & Bacon.

Miettinen, R. (2000). The concept of experiential learning and John Dewey's theory of reflective thought and action. *International Journal of Lifelong Education, 19,* 54.

Mitchell, L. C. (2004). Making the most of creativity in activities for young children with disabilities. *Young Children, 59,* 46–49.

National Center for History in the Schools. (1994). *National standards for history for grades K–4: Expanding children's world in time and space.* Los Angeles, CA: Author.

National Council for the Social Studies. (1994). *Curriculum standards for social studies: Expectations of excellence.* Silver Spring, MD: Author.

National Council for the Social Studies. (1998). *Social studies for early childhood and elementary school children preparing for the 21st century: A report from the NCSS task force on early childhood/elementary social studies.* Silver Spring, MD: Author.

National Gallery of Art. (1998). *Children's guide: Alexander Calder: 1898–1976.* Washington: DC: Author.

National Research Council. (2000). *From neurons to neighborhoods.* Washington, DC: National Academy Press.

National Research Council (2001). *Eager to learn.* Washington, DC: National Academy Press.

Neugebauer, B. (Ed.). (1987). *Alike and different: Exploring our humanity with young children.* Redmond, WA: Exchange Press.

New, R. S. (1990). Excellent early education: A city in Italy has it. *Young Children, 45,* 4–11.

New, R. S. (1998). Diversity and early childhood education: Making room for everyone. In C. Seefeldt & A. Galper (Eds.), *Continuing issues in early childhood education* (2nd ed., pp. 238–265). Upper Saddle River, NJ: Merrill Prentice Hall.

Perry, J. P. (2003). Making sense of outdoor play. *Young Children, 58,* 26–30.

Piaget, J. (1970). *Science of education and the psychology of the child.* New York: Viking Compass Books.

Piaget, J., & Inhelder, B. (1969). *The psychology of the child.* New York: Basic Books.

Powell, D. R. (1989). Families and early childhood programs. *Research Monographs of the National Association for the Education of Young Children, 3.*

Rivkin, M. (1995). *The great outdoors: Restoring children's right to play outside.* Washington, DC: NAEYC.

Rogoff, B. (1995). Observing sociocultural activity on three planes. In J. Wertach, P. Del Rio, & A. Alverez (Eds.), *Sociocultural studies of the mind.* Cambridge, MA: Harvard University Press.

Sarnecka, B. W., & Gelman, S. (2004). Six does not just mean a lot: Preschoolers see number words as specific. *Cognition, 92,* 329–352.

Scully, P., Seefeldt, C., & Barbour, N. (2003). *Developmental continuity across preschool and primary grades.* Wheaton, MD: Association for Childhood Education International.

Seefeldt, C. (1993). Learning for freedom. *Young Children, 48,* 39–45.

Seefeldt, C. (1995). Art: A serious work. *Young Children, 50,* 39–54.

Seefeldt, C. (2002). *Creating rooms of wonder.* Beltsville, MD: Gryphon House.

Seefeldt, C. (2004). *Social studies for the preschool/primary child.* Upper Saddle River, NJ: Merrill/Prentice Hall.

Seefeldt, C., & Barbour, N. (1998). *Early childhood education: An introduction.* Upper Saddle River, NJ: Merrill/Prentice Hall.

Sims, L. S. (1993). *Romare Bearden.* New York: Rissoli International Publications.

Stevenson, D. L., & Baker, D. P. (1987). The family-school relation and the child's school performance. *Child Development, 58,* 1348–1357.

Stone, S. J., & Glascott, K. (1998). The affective side of science instruction. *Childhood Education, 74,* 102–107.

Strum, C. (2003). Creating parent-teacher dialogue: Intercultrual communication in child care. In C. Copple (Ed.), *A world of different: Readings on teaching young children in a diverse society.* Washington, DC. Author.

Swick, K. J. (1997). Learning about work: Extending learning through an ecological approach. In B. Hatcher & S. S. Beck (Eds.), *Learning opportunities beyond the school* (2nd ed., pp. 37–43). Olney, MD: Association for Childhood Education International.

Swick, K., & Freeman, N. (2004). Nurturing peaceful children to create a caring world: The role of families and communities. *Childhood Education, 81,* 2–8.

Turck, M. S. (2000). *The civil rights movement for kids: A history with 21 activities.* Chicago, IL: Chicago Review Press.

Vygotsky, L. (1978). *Thought and language.* Cambridge, MA: MIT Press.

Vygotsky, L. (1986). *Thought and language* (rev. ed.). Cambridge, MA: MIT Press.

Wardle, F. (2003). Supporting multiracial and multiethnic children and their families. In C. Copple (Ed.), *A world of difference: Readings on teaching young children in a diverse society.* Washington, DC: NAEYC.

Wellhousen, K. (2003). Be it ever so humble: Developing a study of homes for today's diverse society. In C. Copple (Ed.), *A world of difference: Readings on teaching young children in a diverse society.* Washington, DC: NAEYC.

Wright, J. L., & Shade, D. D. (1994). *Young children: Active learners in a technological age.* Washington, DC: NAEYC.

Youniss, J., & Damon, W. (1992). Social construction of Piaget's theory. In H. Beilin & P. B. Pufall (Eds.), *Piaget's theory: Prospects and possibilities.* Hillsdale, NJ: Erlbaum.

Resources

Associations and Other Useful Web Pages

Associations have many resources for teachers. Send an e-mail, use the net, write a post-card, or call the following associations and ask for their free or inexpensive resources for teachers of young children:

American Association for State and Local History
1717 Church St.
Nashville, TN 37203-2991
www.aaslh.org/

American Library Association
Caldecott Award Winners
www.ala.org/alsc/caldecott.html
Coretta Scott King Award Winners
www.ala.org/snt/csking

Association for Childhood Education International
17904 Georgia Avenue, Suite 215
Olney, MD 20832
1-800-423-3563
www.acei.org

CTB/McGraw-Hill LLC
20 Ryan Ranch Rd.
Monterey, CA 93940-5703
www.ctb.com/prekguidelines/

Connect for Kids
www.connectforkids.org

Department of Justice Web Page for Children
www.usdoj.gov/kidspage/bias-k-5/index.htm

An Educator's Guide to Adoption
www.adoptioninformationinstitute.org

Government Documents
www.ourdocuments.gov

Government Printing Office
Washington, DC 20402
www.governmentprintingoffice.org

Kids Voting
www.kidsvotingusa.org

National Archives
Washington, DC 20408
1-800-234-8861
www.nara.gov

National Association for the Education of Young Children
1509 16th St., NW
Washington, DC 20036-1426
e-mail: *membership@naeyc.org*
www.naeyc.org

National Center for History in the Schools
University of California, Los Angeles
10880 Wilshire Blvd., Suite 761
Los Angeles, CA 90024-4108
Fax: 310-825-4723
www.sscnet.ucla.edu/nchs/

National Council for the Social Studies
8555 16th St.
Suite 500
Silver Spring, MD 20910
www.socialstudies.org

National Geographic Society
1145 17th St., N.W.
Washington, DC 20037-4688
www.ngsstore.nationalgeographicsociety

National Wildlife Federation
11100 Wildlife Center Drive
Reston, VA 20190-5362
1-800-822-9919
www.nwf.org/

Operation Respect
www.dontlaugh.org

Smithsonian National Museum of the American Indian Education Web Page
www.AmericanIndian.si.edu

Teaching Tolerance Project
The Southern Poverty Law Center
400 Washington Ave.
Montgomery, AL 36104
teachingtotolerance.org

Your Big Back Yard—a magazine for young children

Follow the Drinking Gourd—Rabbit Ears Video

Index

Aberg, R., 110, 114
Active experiences, 4
  connections to community and home, 30–40
  content and, 7–9
  democracy, 152–164
  diversity, 166–178
  economics, 136–149
  families and, 52–66
  friends, 122–133
  geography, 86–105
  history, 68–84
  interactive, 9–10
  language and, 10
  learning continuity, 11–12
  learning environment, 16–28
  mapping, 108–120
  personal meaning, 4–7
  reflection and, 12–13
  social studies, 42–48
  summary, 13–14
Ada, A. F., 19
Adler, D. A., 153, 159
Adoff, A., 54, 59
Adults, interactions with, 10
Aesthetics, 18
African Americans, books related to, 79
Age appropriateness, 6–7
Aliki, 123, 127
American Association for State and Local History
    (AASLH), 69
Ames, L. B., 43
Andersen, B., 70, 78
Animals, 95–96
Antibias music program, 169
Art activities, 25
Art centers. 18–19
Assessment
  democracy, 154
  diversity, 170
  economics, 138–139
  families and, 56
  friends, 125
  geography, 89
  history, 70–71
  mapping, 110
Attitudes, toward families, 55
Authority, 45

Baez, J., 169
Baker, D. P., 39
Bang, M., 123
Barbour, N., 11, 17, 18
Barter exchanges, 141
Batey, J. J., 22
Baylor, B., 89, 96
Beaty, J. J., 19
Beauty, 18
Berg, A., 137
Berg Bochner, A., 137
Berk, L. E., 27, 30
Bhavnagri, N. P., 18
Bisgaier, C. S., 19
Bjorkman, S., 153
Blaska, J. K., 19
Blended family, 52
Block areas, 22
Blocks, 109–110
Blood, P., 142
Bodrova, E., 9
Book centers, 19–20
Books. *See* Children's books; Reference books
Box, J. A., 9
Bredekamp, S.
  connections, 37, 39
  experiences, 5, 7, 10
  social studies, 43, 48
Brill, M. T., 69, 78
Bronfenbrenner, U., 30
Brown, M., 53, 137, 140
Bruner, J., 11
Bryan, A., 169
Bullard, S., 166
Burleigh, R., 79
Burton, V. L., 69, 76
Burts, D. C., 7
Byrnes, D. A., 166

Carle, E., 113
Carnes, J., 166
Casbergue, R. M., 26
Cassatt, M., 60
Cassidy, D. J., 7
Center for Health Statistics, 52
Chalufour, I., 22
Charlesworth, R., 7

Chesanow, N., 110
Children
    characteristics of, 42–43, 45–46
    democracy and, 155–161
    diversity and, 170–175
    economics and, 139–144
    families and, 56–64
    friends, 125–131
    geography and, 90–99
    history and, 71–79
    mapping and, 110–115
Children's Book Council, 69
Children's books, 37
    diversity, 168–169
    economics, 137
    families and, 53–55
    friends, 123–124
    geography, 88–89, 110
    history, 69, 78, 79
Children's museums, 38–39
Choices, 5–6, 139–140
Classrooms, observing and recording changes in, 75–76
Clay, J. W., 52
Clidas, J., 110, 114
Cohen, C. L., 110, 113
Cohen, M., 123, 126
Colker, L. J., 23, 59
Collins, J., 169
Color, 110–112
Commune di Reggio Emilia, 11
Communication, between teachers and families, 55
Community connections, 33, 35–40
Community trips, 37
Computer stations, 23
Concepts
    democracy, 152
    diversity, 166–167
    economics, 136
    families and, 53
    friends, 122–123
    geography, 86
    history, 68
    mapping, 108–109
Conclusions. *See* Reaching conclusions
Conflict resolution, 128–129
Connections, 30–31
    field experiences, 33–35
    neighborhood and community, 33, 35–40
    schools, 31–32
    summary, 40
    See also Home-school connection
Consumption, 140–141
Content, 7–9, 43–46
Continuity, of learning, 11–12
Cooking spaces, 23
Cooper, F., 169
Cooper, J., 9
Cooperation, outdoor opportunities for, 24

Copple, C.
    connections, 37, 39
    diversity, 166
    experiences, 7
    families and, 53
    social studies, 43
Cox, J., 54, 63
CTB, 125
CTB curriculum standards. *See* Curriculum standards
Cultural diversity, 170–172. *See also* Diversity
Culture
    children's books about, 169
    families and, 52–53
    history and, 79
Curriculum standards
    democracy, 152
    diversity, 166–167
    economics, 136
    families and, 53
    friends, 122–123
    geography, 86
    history, 68
    mapping, 108–109
Curtis, J. L., 58
Czernecki, S., 137

Damon, D., 79
Damon, W., 30
Data collection, 76–77
Davidson, E., 166
Davol, M., 54, 59
Decision making, 5–6, 155–157
Democracy, 35–36, 152
    curriculum standards and key concepts, 152
    decision making, 155–157
    documentation, 160–161
    evaluation and assessment, 154
    goals and objectives, 153
    home-school connection, 154
    primary grades, 159–160
    reflection, 159
    resources, 153–154
    tear out sheets, 162–164
    voting, 157–159
dePaola, T., 70, 75, 79, 89, 97, 168, 173
Derman-Sparks, L., 37
Dever, M. T., 9
Dewey, J.
    connections, 30, 35, 36–37
    experiences, 4, 5, 6, 9, 10, 12
    learning environment, 16, 28
    social studies, 42
DeWolf, M., 7
Diamond, K. E., 36
Disabilities, children's books about, 168
Diversity, 36–39, 166
    cultural, 170–172
    curriculum standards and key concepts, 166–167

documentation, 175
evaluation and assessment, 170
gender equality, 173–174
goals and objectives, 167
home-school connection, 170
persons with special needs, 172–173
primary grades, 174–175
reflection and reaching conclusions, 174
resources, 167–169
tear out sheets. 176–178
Documentation
democracy, 160–161
diversity, 175
economics, 143–144
families and, 63–64
friends, 130–131
geography, 97–99
history, 79
mapping, 114–115
Documents, democracy-related, 153
Doniger, N., 70
Dylan, B., 169

Earth. *See* geography
Earth surfaces, 91–94
Economics, 136
curriculum standards and key concepts, 136
documentation, 143–144
evaluation and assessment, 138–139
goals and objectives, 136–137
home-school connection, 138
monetary and barter exchanges, 141
primary grades, 143
production and consumption, 140–141
reflection, 142–143
resources, 137–138
tear out sheets, 145–149
wants, needs, and choices, 139–140
work, 142
English, K., 89, 97
Environment. *See* Learning environment
Ets, M. H., 89, 95
Evaluation, 13
democracy, 154
diversity, 170
economics, 138–139
families and, 56
friends, 125
geography, 89
history, 70–71
mapping, 110
Experiences, sensory, 24. *See also* Active experiences
Experiments, 90
Extended families, 52

Families
concepts, goals, and objectives, 53
culture and, 52–53

documentation, 63–64
evaluation and assessment, 56
family structures, 52
features of, 57–59
home-school connection, 39–40, 55–56
observing and recording changes in, 75
primary grades and, 62–63
reflection, 61–62
relationships, 59–61
resources, 53–55
tear out sheets, 64–66
understanding, 56–57
Fanelli, S., 110, 111
Feelings, 127
Feeney, S., 53
Field, E., 113
Field experiences, 33–35
Firsthand experience, 4–5, 46–48
Five-year-old children, 43
Fleming, D., 89, 96
Foran, J., 70, 79
Four-year-old children, 43
Fraden, D., 153
Freeman, D., 113
Freeman, N. K., 39, 53
Friedman, I. R., 54, 59
Friends, 122
conflict resolution, 128–129
curriculum standards and key concepts, 122–123
documentation, 130–131
evaluation and assessment, 125
feelings, 127
goals and objectives, 123
home-school connection, 125
making and keeping, 128
primary grades, 130
reflection and reaching conclusions, 129
resources, 123–125
self-esteem and self-efficacy, 125–127
tear out sheets, 132–133
Fritz, J., 153
Future time, 72–74

Games, for outdoor learning environments, 24
Gans, R., 89, 96
Gardner, H., 23
Garelick, M., 89, 91
Garrison, B., 89, 91
Gartrell, D., 124
Garza, C. L., 60
Gay-headed/unmarried partner families, 52
Gelman, S., 8
Gender equality, 168, 173–174. *See also* Diversity
Geography, 86
curriculum standards and key concepts, 86
documentation, 97–99
earth surfaces, 91–94
evaluation and assessment, 89
goals and objectives, 86–87

Geography (*Continued*)
   plants and animals, 95–96
   primary grades, 96–97
   reflection, 96
   resources, 87–89
   solar system, 90–91
   tear out sheets, 100–105
   water and landform characteristics, 94–95
George, J. C., 70, 72
Georgetown University Child Development Center, 53
Gesell, A., 43
Glascott, K., 24
Glazer, T., 70, 75
Global connections, 45
Goals
   democracy, 153
   diversity, 167
   economics, 136–137
   families and, 53
   friends, 123
   geography, 86–87
   history, 68
   mapping, 109
Godfrey, N. S., 137
Goleman, D., 39
Governance, 45. *See also* Democracy
Grolnick, W. S., 39
Group work, 9–10

Hakem, J., 160
Hallinan, P. K., 124
Hamanaka, S., 54
Hart, C. H., 7
Hartle, L. C., 22
Havill, J., 124
Health, 16–17
Hearne, B., 70, 78
Hennessy, B. G., 110
Hernandez Sheets, R., 166
Hirsch, E. S., 22
History, 68
   curriculum standards and key concepts, 68
   documentation, 79
   evaluation and assessment, 70–71
   goals and objectives, 68
   home-school connection, 70
   observation and data collection, 76–77
   passage of time changes, 74–76
   passage of time measurements, 71–72
   past, present, and future time, 72–74
   primary grades and, 78–79
   reflection and reaching conclusions, 77–78
   resources, 69–70
   tear out sheets, 80–84
Hoban, L., 130
Hoban, R., 130
Hofer, M., 166

Hoffman, M., 168, 171
Home-school connection, 39–40
   democracy, 154
   diversity, 170
   economics, 138
   families and, 55–56
   friends, 125
   geography and, 89
   history, 70
   mapping, 110
Honigman, J. J., 18
Hornstein, J., 18
Hutchins, P., 70, 75

Igus, T., 54, 55
Ilg, F., 43
Inclusion, planning for, 17
Indoor learning environment, 18–23
Inhelder, B., 5, 9, 10, 47
Initiative, 5–6
Integrity, content with, 7–9
Interactive experiences, 9–10

Jacob, L., 91
Jeffers, S., 143
Jenkins, E., 169
Johnson, A., 54, 63, 70, 75, 124
Jose, A. W., 110

Katz, L., 27
Kaufman, H. O., 55
Keats, E. J., 124, 127
Kellogg, S., 124
Kelso, R., 70, 78
Kemple, K. M., 22
Kieff, J., 26
Kiger, G., 166
Kissinger, K., 174
Kransy, L., 53
Krull, K., 142, 169
Kuhn, D., 137

Laboratory, for geography, 87
Landform characteristics, 94–95
Language, experiences and, 10
Learning, continuity of, 11–12. *See also* Assessment;
       Documentation; Evaluation
Learning environment, 16
   beauty/aesthetics, 18
   families and, 55
   health and safety, 16–17
   inclusion, 17
   indoor spaces, 18–23
   outdoor activity, 25–26
   outdoor spaces, 23–24
   physical activity, 24–25

summary, 27–28
teacher's role, 26–27
Learning experiences. *See* Active experiences
Leedy, L., 110
Leong, D. J., 5, 9, 42
Lesbian-headed/unmarried partner families, 52
Levin, D. E., 9
Lewis, R., 54, 58
Libraries, 37–38
Library centers, 19–20
Lines, 110–112
Lionni, L., 113
Little, D. C., 9
Loughlin, C., 17
Lynch, E. C., 19

MacHotka, H., 137
Mallory, B. L., 18, 36
Mandelbaum, P., 54
Manipulatives, areas for, 21
Mapping, 108
    curriculum standards and key concepts, 108–109
    documentation, 114–115
    evaluation and assessment, 110
    goals and objectives, 109
    home-school connection, 110
    lines, color, and symbols, 110–112
    perspective, 113–114
    primary grades, 114
    reflection, 114
    resources, 109–110
    scale, 112–113
    tear out sheets, 115–120
Marcon, R, A., 39
Martin, B., Jr., 168, 172
Math, outdoor activities, 26
Matlock, R., 18
McAfee, O., 5, 42
McCloskey, R., 89, 97, 113
McMillan, B., 137
McPhail, D. M., 70
Meaning
    content with, 7–9
    personal, 4–7
Miettinen, R., 4, 12, 42
Milne, A. A., 70, 76, 154, 157
Mims, S., 7
Mitchell, L. C., 17
Monetary exchanges, 141
Morgan, W., 169
Movement areas, 22–23
Multiculturalism, children's books about, 168
Murphy, S. J., 110, 114
Museums, 38–39
Music activities, 26
Music areas, 22–23
Music programs, 169

Nathan, A., 137
National Center for History in the School (NCHS), 68, 69
National Children's Book Council, 79
National Council for the Social Studies (NCSS), 8, 44, 69, 136, 152
National Gallery of Art, 38
National Research Council (NRC), 7, 9
Native Americans, children's books about, 79, 169
Natural environment, 32
Needs, 139–140
Neighborhood
    connections with, 33, 35–40
    observing and recording changes in, 75–76
Neugebauer, B., 61
New, R. S., 18, 37
Newman, L., 54

Objectives
    democracy, 153
    diversity, 167
    economics, 136–137
    families and, 53
    friends, 123
    geography, 86–87
    history, 68
    mapping, 109
Observation
    history, 74–77
    outdoor learning environments, 24
O'Connor, J., 50
Organized games, for outdoor learning environments, 24
Organizing, 12–13
Osborne, M. P., 70, 79
Outdoor activity, 25–26
Outdoor learning environment, 23–24, 32

Palen, D., 137
Parents, 39–40, 52. *See also* Families
Parkinson, K., 53
Parnall, P., 70, 76
Past time, 72–74
Patterson, A., 142
Pellegrini, N., 54
People, observing and recording changes in, 75–76
Perry, J. P., 9
Personal meaning, 4–7
Persons with special needs, 172–173. *See also* Diversity
Perspective, 109, 113–114
Physical activity, 24–25
Piaget, J.
    connections, 30
    experiences, 5, 9, 10
    social studies, 42, 47
Plants, 95–96
Play, 9
Polk, N., 166
Potter, B., 113

Powell, D. R., 39
Power, 45
Prejudice, children's books about, 168
Present time, 72–74
Primary grades
    democracy, 159–160
    diversity, 174–175
    economics, 143
    families and, 62–63
    friends, 130
    geography, 96–97
    history, 78–79
    mapping, 114
Production, 140–141
Projects, 9–10

Quiet spaces, 23

Rabe, T., 110
Rappaport, D., 168
Raschka, C., 169
Reaching conclusions
    diversity, 174
    friends, 129
    history, 76–78
Reference books
    democracy, 153–154
    economics, 137
Reflection
    democracy, 159
    diversity, 174
    economics, 142–143
    experiences, 12–13
    families and, 61–62
    friends, 129
    geography, 96
    history, 76–78
    mapping, 114
Relationships, 59–61. *See also* Connections; Families
Resources
    democracy, 153–154
    diversity, 167–169
    economics, 137–138
    families and, 53–55
    friends, 123–125
    geography, 87–89
    history, 69–70
    mapping, 109–110
Rhodes, T., 137
Ringgold, F., 168, 169, 171
Rohmann, E., 124, 127
Rosegrant, T., 10, 48
Ross, D., 124
Rucker, L., 7

Safety, 16–17, 34
Samaras, T., 19

Sand areas, 22
Sand tables, 87–88
Sarnecka, B. W., 8
Say, A., 168
Scale, 108, 112–113
Schaefer, A. R., 60
Schniedewind, N., 166
School building, 32
Schools, 31–32. *See also* Home-school
        connection
Schwartz, D., 137
Science
    outdoor activities, 25
    social studies and, 45
Science areas, 21–22
Scully, P., 11
Seefeldt, C.
    connections, 33, 36, 39
    experiences, 6, 11
    families and, 61
    learning environment, 16, 17, 18
Self-efficacy, 125–127
Self-esteem, 125–127
Sendak, M., 113
Sensory experiences, 24
Shade, D. D., 23
Shiller, P. B., 70, 75
Silberg, J., 70, 75
Sims, L. S., 172
Single parents, 52
Sisulu, E., 154, 157
Skutch, R., 54, 55
Slowiaczek, M. L., 39
Smith, C. L., 54, 61
Social class, children's books about, 169
Social studies, 42–48. *See also* Democracy; Diversity;
        Economics; Families; Friends; Geography; History;
        Mapping
Society, 45
Sociodramatic play activities, 25
Sociodramatic play areas, 20–21
Solar system, 90–91
Soman, D, 75
Special needs. *See* Persons with special needs
Stacey, S., 36
Steptoe, J., 54, 70, 79
Stevenson, D. L., 39
Stone, S. J., 24
Sturm, C., 56
Subject matter knowledge, 43–46
Suina, J., 17
Supplies, for history, 69
Swick, K. J., 36, 39
Symbols, 110–112

Taberski, S., 70, 72
Taylor, M. D., 70

Teachers
 democracy, 152–154
 diversity, 166–170
 economics, 136–139
 families and, 52–56
 friends, 122–125
 geography, 86–89
 history, 68–71
 interactions with, 10
 learning environment, 26–27
 mapping, 108–110
Tear out sheets
 democracy, 162–164
 diversity, 176–178
 economics, 145–149
 families and, 65–66
 friends and, 132–133
 geography, 100–105
 history, 80–84
 mapping, 115–120
Technology, 45
Thomas, J. C., 75
Three-year-old children, 42
Time
 measuring passage of, 71–72
 past, present, and future, 72–74
 recording changes, 74–76
Turck, M. S., 160, 166

Udry, J. M., 1324, 128

Van Leeuwen, J., 70, 78
Videos, diversity-related, 169

Viorst, J., 137
Visitors, 37
Voting, 157–159
Vygotsky, L.
 connections, 30
 experiences, 5, 9, 10
 learning environment, 21, 27
 social studies, 47

Walker, S. M., 70, 77
Wants, 139–140
Wardle, F., 52
Water areas, 22
Water characteristics, 94–95
Water tables, 87–88
Websites, diversity-related, 169
Wellhousen, K., 56
Wells, R., 70, 72, 79, 137, 142
Wells, T., 70, 79
Wilhoite, M., 55
Williams, V., 137
Winsler, A., 27, 30
Woodson, J., 55, 62
Work, 142
Worth, K., 22
Wright, D. C., 70, 75
Wright, J. L., 23
Wyeth, S. D., 70, 76

Yarrow, P., 124
Youniss, J., 30
Yurchenko, H., 169

Zolotow, C., 124, 127